SAXON SHORE

BRANCASTER
BURGH CASTLE
CAISTER
CAMBRIDGE
WALTON CASTLE
COLCHESTER
BRADWELL
RECULVER
PICKBOROUGH
DOVER
LYMPNE
BOULOGNE
PEVENSEY
LONDON
WATLING ST.
STANE STREET
CHICHESTER
ST. ALBANS
ERMINE STREET
LEICESTER
WINCHESTER
SILCHESTER
CIRENCESTER
AKEMAN STREET
FOSSE WAY
BATH
PORCHESTER
DORCHESTER
GLOUCESTER
CAERLEON
WATLING STREET
WROXETER
CAERNARVON
CARDIFF
EXETER

FORTRESSES
FORTS (LATE MAINLY)
NAVIGABLE WATERWAYS

C0-BIG-159

THE STORY OF ROMAN BRITAIN

By

D. R. BARKER

Illustrated by

JOHN LATHEY, M.S.I.A.

ST. MARTIN'S PRESS

NEW YORK

Library of Congress Catalog Card Number: 63/13668

Made and printed in
Great Britain by
FLETCHER AND SON LTD NORWICH

PREFACE

The Story of Roman Britain is intended for children aged from ten to fourteen. It is a very small book and obviously cannot tell the full story of Britain when she was a part of the Roman Empire. In fact no attempt has been made to write an outline history of Roman Britain. Instead some material has been deliberately excluded in order that more important or interesting aspects of the subject might be covered more fully. It is hoped that the use of detail in this book will arouse the interest of children and lead them on to read more widely about the subject in larger books.

The omission of some details of the military campaigns, for example, has allowed a large section of the book to be devoted to a description of the towns—defences, great public buildings, houses, street systems and people. But only a small proportion of the population lived in towns, most lived in the countryside and worked the land as their ancestors had done and as their descendants were to do for many hundreds of years. The Story of Roman Britain includes a full account of country life: farming and farming implements; the peasant's hut and the great villa; the various small industries that grew up wherever there were plentiful supplies of timber, good clay, or valuable minerals. There is also a lengthy description of the various religions and cults of the province in which special emphasis has been laid on the cult of Mithras and the growth of Christianity during the last century of Roman rule.

Throughout the book an attempt has been made to incorporate the latest evidence provided by archaeological research.

I would like to thank my friend Mr. J. Harding for reading the manuscript and making many valuable suggestions.

D.R.B.

ACKNOWLEDGEMENTS

THE Author and Publisher wish to acknowledge the kind permission given by William Heinemann Ltd. to quote from *Lullingstone Roman Villa* by Lt.-Col. G. W. Meates; Penguin Books Ltd. to quote from *Bede* by Leo Sherley-Price; Frederick Muller Ltd. to quote from *Arthur and his Times* by Jack Lindsay; Max Parrish & Co. Ltd. to include information on Silchester from *Roman Silchester* by G. C. Boon.

THE MUTINY

By the time of the death of Christ most of western Europe was under Roman domination. From the coasts of conquered Gaul, however, the Romans still looked across to the free island of Britain which had given JULIUS CAESAR'S armies such a shock when they had invaded it nearly a century before. Julius Caesar had failed, but his description of Britain had aroused much interest in Rome, and from that time onwards it was generally accepted that it was only a question of time before the island was occupied. In 43 A.D. CLAUDIUS, the new emperor, decided that the time was ripe, and four legions were ordered to the port of Boulogne to embark in the invasion fleet.

The Roman legions always needed careful handling and now, when they received their orders to leave their comfortable quarters, they flatly refused and broke out in open mutiny. The legionaries were not at all impressed by the fact that the turbulent Britons were raiding the coasts of Gaul, nor that Britain's wealth in gold, silver and lead would flow into the coffers of Rome. They said they were quite comfortable where they were, and saw no reason why they should risk their lives crossing an ocean to fight painted savages in an island on the very edge of the known world. Moreover they reminded each other that when the previous emperor had been assassinated, Claudius had been found trembling behind a curtain; now, no doubt, he was trying to make people forget the humiliating start to his reign by covering himself with glory at their expense. The great Caesar had taken five legions to Britain and had been lucky to get back alive. If Caesar failed, what chance had weak-kneed and feeble-minded Claudius?

The Emperor Claudius.
(Photo: Mansell Collection)

Even the prospect of loot for themselves failed to make the legions change their minds, and in the end Claudius had to send his chief secretary, a man called Narcissus, to talk to them. At first Narcissus made matters worse, for the legionaries resented a man who was an ex-slave, a Greek and a civilian, lecturing them on their duty to the emperor. Eventually, however, as they saw the ex-slave puffing out his chest and strutting about as if he was the emperor himself, their sense of humour got the better of them, the whole army roared with laughter, and Aulus Plautius, the very efficient commander, managed to restore order. There was no more trouble and the troops quietly embarked.

BRITAIN AT THIS TIME

THE Roman impression that Britain was inhabited by ignorant painted savages was not correct. Its people were capable of superb craftsmanship in metal and wood, and in many ways their native art was infinitely superior to that of the Romans. The southern part of Britain, moreover, was dominated by powerful BELGIC tribes (originally from Belgium). These tribes were under Roman influence and were importing Roman objects on a large scale. They issued their own coinage and built tribal capitals, which in time might have developed into proper towns. Their farmers were so skilful that Britain was able to export wheat.

Yet there is no doubt that even the Belgae were ferocious and in many ways primitive. Their chieftains might drink themselves into a daze with delicate Italian wines out of the finest Gallic cups, but their huts had earthen floors and were filled with smoke unable to find its way out through the hole in the roof. A Belgic chieftain came home from a raid on a neighbouring tribe in a chariot brilliant with red and blue enamelled fittings, the bronze trappings of the horses jingling, but from the bridle there hung the dripping heads of his enemies. These later adorned temples or the gateways of forts. Their priests, the Druids, prophesied by stabbing a man in the back and noting his convulsions.

Their ferocity made the Britons formidable enemies. A charge by a screaming horde of their warriors must have been just as devastating to an undisciplined enemy as one by BONNIE PRINCE CHARLIE'S Highlanders. Moreover the Britons still used the warchariot which had gone out of use in the rest of Europe. This could be very effective against an inexperienced enemy, for the mere sight of several hundred chariots coming straight at them was enough to make many opponents break ranks and flee. If they stood firm they were subjected to a rain of missiles from the occupants of the chariots. There is no evidence to show that these chariots were ever equipped with swords on their axles (all thoughts of Boudicca's chariots neatly lopping off Romans at the knees must be relinquished), but even without whirling swords these chariots were formidable weapons.

Yet Britain was militarily weak. The Belgic tribes who dominated the south were, it is true, superb fighters, but their aggression had infuriated their neighbours, and many of them were only awaiting a chance to stab the Belgae in the back. When the Romans landed these tribes remained neutral and refused to help the Belgae, who bore the brunt of the early fighting; sometimes they actually assisted the Romans. Moreover in any set battle the wild, unorganized fury of the British tribes was no match for the methodical and disciplined skill of the Romans. How very great were the odds against the Britons can be seen by an examination of the Roman army of invasion.

THE ROMAN ARMY

FOUR legions drawn from Gaul and central Europe made up the main strength of the Roman army invading Britain. Each of these legions was made up of over 5,000 professional soldiers who had enlisted for at least twenty years, and who had spent the whole of their time learning the craft of war. It is hardly surprising that a legion was usually more than a match for any equal number of opponents.

Under his drill master the legionary learned to use his short sword by practising against stakes or against other legionaries. He was taught how to throw a javelin in full armour, using sods of grass or a stake as a target. Together with the other legionaries he learned how to fight his way out of ambushes, how to repel sudden attacks, and how to form the 'tortoise' by linking his shield with those of his companions. He was toughened up by frequent route marches of twenty miles, during which the pace was varied from a natural march to a rapid trot. He was also employed in building practice-camps, bridges and roads. The engineering skill he obtained from this kind of work frequently stood him in good stead in time of war, and helped to civilize many a conquered province.

The legionary owed a part of his success in battle to his equipment. On his right side he carried a two-foot sword with a blade of wrought iron. This was used for stabbing rather than slashing, and was very useful when the legionary was fighting at close quarters. For long-distance fighting he carried a javelin. This weapon had only the head tempered, the rest of the iron shaft being left soft. As a result, when the point pierced an enemy's shield the shaft bent, and the enemy had an awkward encumbrance attached to his shield. Caesar in one of his histories tells us what then happened. 'Many of the Gauls were struck by the first discharge of weapons, and as the iron had become bent they were unable to draw them out, nor could they fight conveniently with their left arm thus additionally encumbered.' So they did just what the Romans wanted them to do—they threw their shields away.

The legionary's armour gave him good protection. A bronze helmet with a neck-guard and face-pieces took the force of the slashing down stroke of the barbarian's long sword; back and

A heavy catapult in action.

chest were protected by a pair of plates and a system of overlapping strips. On his left arm the legionary carried a large rectangular shield made of pieces of wood covered with hides and strengthened by an iron boss and rim.

The normal custom in battle was for the legionaries to open the attack with a discharge from the legionary catapults and a volley of javelins. While the enemy was still disorganized, the legionaries advanced in close order with their shields almost meeting. When they came to close quarters the legionary's short sword usually proved far more effective than the native's long sword: the barbarian's sword swung, in thrust the short sword, and the legionary pushed forward over the body of his enemy.

Arms and equipment, however, only partly account for the efficiency of the Roman army. Much of its success was due to the severity with which discipline was enforced. Units which had deserted on the field of battle sometimes had every tenth man executed, the unfortunate men being stoned to death by their own comrades. The same fate befell sentries who fell asleep on duty. Less serious offences were punished by flogging or by loss of pay.

Discipline was normally enforced by the CENTURIONS. These officers formed the backbone of the Roman army. They might at times be far too willing to use their vine staffs on the backs of recruits, and there is no doubt that many legionaries were able to bribe them to let them off undesirable fatigues, but their value to the Roman army was so great that they were paid approximately twelve times as much as ordinary rankers. Whereas the higher officers were merely amateurs, who had to complete three years military service before they could pursue a more profitable career, the centurions, many of whom had risen from the ranks, often served twenty to thirty years, and thus acquired a far more detailed knowledge of military matters than their superiors.

A Roman army on the march.

Each centurion commanded a century of eighty men (not a hundred as might well be thought), and was responsible for their training and discipline. These were, however, not his only duties, for quite often he was left in charge of garrisons, and sometimes he was given command of legionary detachments. The senior centurions, moreover, were often invited to military councils where their experience would be useful when tactics and strategy were discussed. Men in a position like this had to possess a keen intelligence and a strong personality; most centurions were probably well worth their high rate of pay.

The one great weakness of the Roman army was its lack of cavalry. It is true that each legion was equipped with 120 horsemen, but they were mainly occupied with scouting and dispatch duties, and much of the normal work of cavalry was done by AUXILIARY units—what we would call native troops—commanded by a Roman officer. Auxiliaries were also employed as infantry.

A Roman army on the march must have been an impressive sight. First came swarms of auxiliary horse sweeping over the countryside and scouring the territory for enemies in ambush. Then, slowly, plodding, with full equipment, the engineers who cleared the way for the rest of the army and who that night would set out the camp within its ramparts. Next, with a flash of colour, came the commander with his bodyguard in polished armour, and the legionary horse. Behind them, ploughing deep into the ground, rumbled the siege train: rams with iron heads; 'wild asses', the heavy catapults which could throw a 2 cwt. boulder 500 yards; and in their pony carts the quick-firing, light catapults with their barrels of bolts. Finally came the standard bearers marching proudly in their bearskins, standards erect, and the great mass of the legionaries, each man carrying his saw, basket, pickaxe, mess-tin, kettle and three days' rations, in addition to sword, javelins, shield and

9

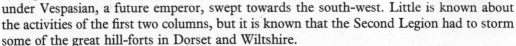

full armour. Centurions marched behind to prevent men from
falling out.

It was an army of this kind that was about to confront the amateur
warriors of Britain and was to play so great a part in the history of
the country during more than three hundred years.

THE EARLY CAMPAIGNS IN BRITAIN

THE army sailed in three convoys and landed in Kent. Resistance in
the south-east was overcome, the Thames crossed and Colchester,
the Belgic capital, captured. The army was then divided into three
sections: the Ninth Legion struck north and built a fortress at
Lincoln; the Fourteenth and the Twentieth Legions pressed
through the heavily-forested Midlands; and the Second Legion
under Vespasian, a future emperor, swept towards the south-west. Little is known about
the activities of the first two columns, but it is known that the Second Legion had to storm
some of the great hill-forts in Dorset and Wiltshire.

One of these hill-forts, MAIDEN CASTLE, covered nearly a hundred acres and had
several rows of ramparts separated by ditches cut out of the solid chalk. Each rampart rose
sheer, buttressed by timber and stone and was topped by a timber palisade. The inner
rampart rose to a height of 50 feet above its ditch. These multiple ramparts were probably designed as a defence against the sling, which was the chief missile weapon used
in southern Britain; hoards of over 20,000 sling-stones have been found in Maiden Castle
itself.

The Second Legion came up against Maiden Castle in A.D. 45. It probably presented few
problems to the Romans, for they excelled in siege-craft and always preferred to come up
against solid resistance rather than a will-o'-the-wisp enemy. If the attack was mounted
in the normal fashion the catapults were clamped to their timber emplacements, the
auxiliary slingers and archers swarmed up the hill, and soon the 'wild asses' began to
kick and the quick-firers began to screech and a rain of boulders, bolts and arrows descended
upon the inhabitants of the fortress. Anyone who showed himself above the level of the
rampart was immediately picked off. We know what happened next: under cover of this
intense fire the legionaries worked their way up the hill, set light to the east gate and
forced their way into the fortress. The defenders fought so hard that they infuriated the
Romans, who continued to cut and slash at them when they were quite dead. A halt was
eventually called to the massacre and the survivors were allowed to bury their dead. When
the cemetery was excavated recently one of the skeletons still had a Roman catapult bolt
firmly fixed in his spine.

Four years after the Roman landing in Britain most of the lowland had been conquered,
and a Roman frontier road, the FOSSE WAY, ran from Lincoln in the north-east to near
Exeter in the south-west.

A QUEEN REVOLTS

FOR several years the Fosse Way marked the frontier of Roman Britain, but in the late
fifties the advance began again, with the Romans trying to conquer northern Wales and
Anglesey, a stronghold of the Druids. Anglesey had just been taken when the Roman commander, SUETONIUS PAULINUS, received news that the whole of eastern Britain was

in revolt and that Colchester, where Roman veterans had been settled, had been sacked and its citizens put to death with savage tortures. What was far worse the Ninth Legion bravely marching down from Lincoln, had been surprised and practically annihilated.

The tribe in revolt was the *ICENI*. Originally this tribe had been friendly with the Romans, and in fact had been among the first tribes to make peace with the invaders. The Iceni had, however, been treated abominably and in A.D. 60 when their king died the Romans had confiscated the royal family's property and much of that belonging to the nobility. The royal palace was looted and, a crowning insult, BOUDICCA, the queen, flogged. The tribe outraged at this insult to their queen had broken out in spontaneous revolt and had carried other tribes with them. By the time Suetonius received the news the Iceni, triumphant after their successes against Colchester and the Ninth Legion, were moving rapidly towards a defenceless London.

Suetonius ordered the Second Legion to march from the south-west, but it refused, and Suetonius' own legions were unable to reach the city in time. A screaming horde descended upon London, sacked it, and massacred the inhabitants. The same fate befell St. Albans. The bones of some of the 70,000 who died at this time are still occasionally found by workmen excavating in the City of London, and both at London and St. Albans layers of ashes many feet below the present ground surface, reveal to archaeologists the fate of the two cities.

Somewhere in the Midlands Boudicca's tribesmen met the Roman army under Suetonius Paulinus. The Romans numbered 10,000, the Britons perhaps five times that number. Boudicca, her yellow hair streaming, rode up and down the ranks of her warriors reminding them of their wrongs and exhorting them to crush the rule of the Romans in Britain. Confident of victory the tribes came out in front of their wagons to offer battle, whilst the children and womenfolk screamed encouragement.

Suetonius had chosen his position carefully so that his flanks were protected by thick forest, and this meant that the Britons had to make a frontal attack. The Romans stood firm and then, when the enemy was within range, hurled their javelins. 10,000 of these descended upon the Britons within a few seconds and, while the Britons were still reeling, the trumpets sounded and Roman horse and infantry charged together and swept them back against their wagons. The gaps between the wagons were soon blocked with bodies and the Britons, now a confused, struggling mass, were slaughtered in their thousands. Boudicca fled and took poison; and at Gloucester the commander of the Second Legion fell on his sword.

THE WALL

AFTER the country had been completely pacified a succession of vigorous and able governors resumed the advance. Wales and northern England were conquered and held down by forts and fortresses, and the Roman forces advanced into Scotland. Much of lowland Scotland was conquered, but the withdrawal of one legion from the garrison of Britain forced the Romans to halt their forward policy and give up many of their gains in the

The Emperor Hadrian.
(Photo: Mansell Collection)

On watch along Hadrian's Wall.

north. They were further crippled when, in the early second century, the Ninth Legion suffered such a severe defeat that it disappeared from history. The situation in the north became so chaotic that no less a person than the Emperor HADRIAN himself had to come to Britain to try to find a solution to the problem.

Hadrian decided that the great need in the North was a definite frontier, which would establish once and for all where barbarian territory finished and where Roman territory began. The frontier should have fortifications strong enough to resist tribal infiltrations and raids. It was finally decided that a wall should be built.

When finished Hadrian's Wall stretched for 73 miles between the mouth of the Tyne and Solway Firth. In its final form it was stone built, varied in width from 7 to 10 feet and stood with its parapet 21 feet high. In front of it ran a 30-foot ditch. The Wall was equipped with fortlets every mile and turrets every third of a mile. At irregular intervals were sixteen larger forts, some garrisoned with cavalry, some with infantry and some with both. The garrison for the whole Wall probably amounted to nearly 16,000 men, a third of the total garrison of Britain.

Some forts were built well in advance of the Wall to help to break up concentrations of the enemy, and warn the Wall garrison when trouble was coming. They also acted as bases for scouts, who roamed all over the Highlands obtaining information and delivering messages. These forts were heavily fortified and were equipped with catapults, for their position was a very exposed and dangerous one (very similar to that of forts established in Indian territory in nineteenth-century America).

Behind Hadrian's Wall ran a road connecting the Wall forts, and farther back, at a distance ranging from a few yards to half a mile, another ditch, usually known as the Vallum. The purpose of this ditch is unknown, but it may have been the southern boundary of a military zone into which unauthorized persons were not allowed to enter. This precaution would help to prevent sudden and surprise attacks on the rear from natives pretending to be friendly.

The new defences were a success. One of the northern forts—perhaps Bewcastle, Netherby or Birrens—would receive news that a raiding party was on its way south; the signal fires would be lit and their warning smoke sent swirling into the sky. Soon the trumpets would shrill the alarm along the Wall, and in the forts all would be bustle and noise as the garrisons prepared for war. In a few minutes the Wall would be manned and the cavalry streaming out through the great double gateways of the forts. Tribesmen hoping to slip quickly and quietly through the defences must have been horrified when they

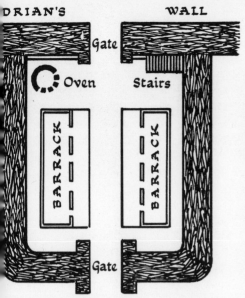

Gate

Oven   Stairs

BARRACK   BARRACK

Gate

A milecastle on Hadrian's Wall.

found the Wall bristling with soldiers, and the Roman cavalry bearing down hard upon them. Many a raider at times like this must have vowed that in future he would be content with his own cattle.

The success of Hadrian's Wall led to an attempt to repeat the same scheme of defence farther north, by building a wall between the Firth of Forth and the Clyde. This wall, however, could not be held, for the distance between the two walls was too large to be controlled, with the result that the tribes behind the northern wall were just as dangerous to it as those in front. This wall was consequently abandoned at the end of the second century after it had twice been overrun, and Hadrian's Wall remained the northern frontier of the province throughout the next two centuries of the Roman occupation.

FORTS AND FORTRESSES

BEHIND the Wall, forts held down the newly conquered parts of Britain. These forts, like the Wall, were garrisoned by auxiliaries, whose main task was to police the area around them and stop hit-and-run raids. The main responsibility for dealing with large invasions fell on the three legions. The Sixth Legion (this had replaced the unfortunate Ninth) guarded the north from its fortress at York (Eboracum), and the Twentieth and the Second, from their bases at Chester (Deva) and Caerleon (Isca), kept watch on the routes from North and South Wales.

Both the auxiliary forts and the legionary fortresses were rectangular in shape with rounded corners, but the fortresses, covering 50 to 60 acres, were usually five or six times the size of the forts. They were heavily defended. An enemy approaching one of them from the outside would have to cross a wide, deep ditch, sometimes planted with quickthorn, the Roman equivalent of barbed wire, or cut so that its outer face was vertical whilst the inner side was gently sloping; the attacker could easily jump on to the inner slope, but when he tried to retreat he had to climb up the vertical outside face, presenting a broad back as a target for the defenders. Occasionally, as an additional defence, pits were dug and furnished with pointed stakes. The pits were then covered up with brushwood and grass. They must have had a devastating effect on a charge by unsuspecting tribesmen.

Behind the ditch came a stone wall backed by a rampart of clay or turf. The wall was equipped with square towers at intervals, and had the corners especially strengthened with timbers and turves to support the heavy catapult known as the 'wild ass'. (The kick from this catapult was so strong that it could shatter a stone base.) Probably the lighter catapults could be mounted anywhere along the ramparts.

Normally forts and fortresses were laid out on roughly the same lines. In the centre was the headquarters building, made up of a great hall, courtyard and the offices of the army clerks. Nearby stood the commander's house and the heavily buttressed granaries; the latter always held enough corn to last the garrison a full year. Much of the rest of the fort or fortress was occupied by long, monotonous rows of barracks, but there were also stables, workshops for the armourers, masons, smiths and carpenters, and, in the case of the fortresses, a hospital for the sick or wounded. Fortresses were also provided with an AMPHITHEATRE where troops could be trained, and baths where they could meet during off-duty hours. All buildings were built neatly of stone, and were laid out according to the precise regulations of the military manuals. All roads crossed at right angles. Forts and fortresses were grey and stark, but grimly impressive.

THE ROADS

ALTHOUGH the bases of the legionaries were heavily fortified, only in cases of extreme emergency did the legions allow themselves to be shut up within their walls. Normally the legions occupied them only during peace-time. As soon as the scouts brought news that the northern tribes were gathering, the signal fires would blaze from Stanwix on the Wall to York, and out would march the Sixth Legion; occasionally if the trouble was really serious it would be reinforced by detachments from the Second and Twentieth Legions. York was a considerable distance from the northern frontier, and the troops had to move quickly if the auxiliaries guarding the frontier were not to be overrun and the peaceful countryside devastated. The Wall, however, was seldom penetrated, for the legions were able to move at great speed along the fine network of roads that covered Britain.

Many of these roads had been built during the time when the legions were still fighting hard to subdue the island. For example WATLING STREET, running from London to the north-west, was probably built by the Twentieth and Fourteenth Legions as they drove through the Midlands, and the road to the North, ERMINE STREET, by the Ninth as it marched towards Lincoln. Over the straight, metalled roads prepared by their engineers these legions were able to roll smoothly forward. The other great main road of Roman Britain, the FOSSE WAY running from near Exeter to Lincoln, was constructed to link up the forts along the frontier-line which defended lowland Britain during the early years of the conquest. As time went by more and more roads were built to link up the various forts and cities that dotted the new province. Many of these later roads, especially the minor ones, must have been built by the civilian authorities, but even so it is probable that they called in the experienced engineers of the legion as advisers.

Road making during the early years must have been a difficult and sometimes perilous task, for the legions were always exposed to the hit-and-run raids of Britons who realized that these great striding roads meant an end to their liberty. Hundreds of years later the North American Indians fought just as desperately against the railroad for the same reasons. However the resistance of the Britons was no more successful than that of the Indians, for most of the great roads were completed within a very few years of the invasion.

The roads were usually made up of straight sections, and sometimes ran for many miles in a straight line across country. Occasionally, a too rigid adherence to this policy led the Roman surveyors to take the roads over steep hills when a detour should have been made. The Roman road into Lincoln, for example, is too steep today for vehicles, and can only be used by walkers, and at Blackstone Edge in Lancashire the road had to be provided

A fast two-horse chariot on a Roman road.

with a central groove for the brake-poles of carts descending the very steep hill. It is by no means true, however, that Roman roads always ran straight, for they often climbed steep slopes by a series of zig-zags, or rounded a hill by means of an 18-foot terrace cut out of the hill-side.

However bad the country, nothing stopped the Roman engineers. The marshy country of the Medway, for instance, was crossed by a 14-foot paved causeway with a foundation of flints, rammed chalk and gravel, all resting on thick oak piles and beams. In Scotland 20-foot roads were driven across peat bogs and straight over the high moors, cuttings being made through the hills. Rivers were crossed by paved fords or by heavy timber bridges with stone foundations. There do not appear to have been any of the great arched bridges of stone, like the Romans built in the more civilized parts of the Empire.

The roads were usually solidly constructed. Sometimes it is true they were made of a single layer of material laid directly on the subsoil, but normally the main roads had a foundation of heavy stones and a surfacing of a finer material like gravel. Good drainage was essential, and the actual road was often laid on an embankment, known by the Romans as an *AGGER*. This was sometimes quite high; Ackling Dyke, the agger of the Roman road between Old Sarum and Badbury Rings in Dorset, is still 6 feet high in places and between

15

40 and 50 feet wide. To throw off surface water the road was sloped from the centre to the outside edges. Sometimes there is a fall of a foot in a 15-foot road.

As today, the widths of roads varied a great deal; some were barely 10 feet wide, whereas Akeman Street, running from St. Albans to Cirencester, had stretches of double carriage-way with a total width of 32 feet.

Throughout the history of Roman Britain, legionaries and auxiliaries passed backwards and forwards along these roads on their way to crush an uprising or defeat an enemy attack; but the same roads were used for far more peaceful purposes. To the south-coast ports came the iron-shod packhorses carrying the silver and lead of the western Mendips. Over the iron slag roads of Sussex creaked and groaned the heavy wagons carrying wheat and iron to London. From the great villa-estates all over southern Britain came hides, wool and pork for the Roman army, and wheat for the towns. Fine pottery and glassware, carefully crated, and great amphorae, full of the delicate wines of Gaul, travelled these roads on their way to the rich of town and country. Occasionally, with a splash of gravel, there passed by a fast two-horse chariot driven by a rich young Briton, or an Imperial messenger riding a foaming horse. The messengers were able to cover over a hundred miles in a day, for every ten to fifteen miles along the main roads were posting stations where they could obtain fresh horses. Not until the eighteenth century TURNPIKES were built were people again able to travel so easily and at such great speeds.

The British roads, moreover, were only part of a vast network that stretched from the Atlantic to the Euphrates. Along these roads traders and tourists were able to travel freely, without passport or language difficulties, and with them they carried not only goods but ideas. Britons were soon reading the works of the Latin poets and thinking like Romans. The gods of Greece and Rome became theirs, and soon these were joined by those of Egypt and Syria; along the same roads came the news from the East of the man who had died to save all mankind.

THE TOWN IN THE WOODS

THE Roman road from London south-west ran through lonely, heavily-forested country, and did not branch until it reached Silchester, known by the Romans as Calleva Atrebatum, the Town of the Atrebates in the Wood. These ATREBATES were a Belgic tribe that had come to Britain in the first century B.C. and had founded a kingdom which for a time covered the whole of Hampshire and Berkshire and a large part of Surrey. Calleva became their capital. When Vespasian and the Second Legion came that way in A.D. 44 the settlement was defended by great banks and ditches, but there is no evidence of fighting, and perhaps the Atrebates, who were hard pressed by other Belgic tribes, were one of Rome's early allies in Britain.

It was a part of Roman policy to encourage the growth of towns like Silchester. Like the Greeks earlier on, the Romans believed that man was by nature the creature of a city. By the time the Romans came to Britain all the Mediterranean lands were dotted with large cities, and, as these areas were by far the most civilized parts of Europe, there was a natural tendency for the Romans to think that it was the city that civilized a country. To their mind the citizen who lived in a well-ordered city with great colonnaded buildings,

Inside the gateway of a Roman town.

regularly planned streets and comfortable houses, with entertainment provided by the arena and theatre, and with his wits sharpened by good conversation and constant association with other citizens and people from distant places, was a vastly superior being to the peasant, whose mind was narrowed by his struggle for mere existence, and whose only companions were as brutish as himself. In addition the city-dweller, luxuriating in hot and cold baths and living in a comfortable home, became softened, and, even if he did revolt, was not nearly so dangerous as the tough tribesman ranging the wind-swept hills, or stubborn behind the stout ramparts of his hill-fort.

In most cases it was not necessary to use force to compel the tribesmen to abandon their old homes and live in a town. With peace and security there was no need to live in a draughty, waterless hill-fort like Maiden Castle, and every encouragement to move to a lowland town like Dorchester, where a man could flourish under the Roman peace. The peace alone was enough to breed new towns. Britain was connected with the Continent far more closely than ever before, and traders from Italy, Gaul and the East saw in Britain's primitive, gullible tribesmen a wonderful market, and unloaded on them all their defective and out-of-date stock; Britons happily displayed Roman pottery considered old-fashioned for years by the refined citizens of Italy and Gaul. Traders poured into Britain, and as a result of their activity a great city, London, grew up on the banks of the Thames, and within a very short time became the third largest city north of the Alps. At cross roads and at fords, traders and craftsmen built their shacks, and in time their settlements grew into small towns. Farmers, also profiting from the peace, sent their surplus cereals, cattle and pigs to market, and as they grew wealthier, built themselves comfortable houses where they could stay when in town. As a result, by the end of the second century, humble little market-centres like Ilchester had grown into sizable towns. Although it was still largely rural, Britain became dotted with small towns.

Many of the smaller towns no doubt remained very similar to the pre-conquest settlements—unplanned, undrained and rather squalid—but the tribal capitals and other large towns were influenced by places like Colchester, Lincoln or Gloucester, where, for the benefit of legionary veterans, the town was laid out on deliberately Roman lines. Silchester, for example, probably borrowed money, enlisted the aid of the invaluable legionary engineers and architects (many of the civic centres in British towns are modelled on the legionary headquarters building), and soon became a fair imitation of the normal, Roman provincial town.

Few British towns, however, approached the size and population of those in more civilized parts of the Empire. Silchester, which covered 107 acres and was an important road centre, probably never had a population of more than 3,000, and its two hundred houses were widely scattered. Many of its people earned their living by farming the light, gravelly soil around the town, and it is highly probable that cattle and pigs were kept in paddocks within the town walls. Beyond the arable lands stretched miles of uncleared oak forest, where herds of swine were allowed to forage, and where at night wolves howled and bears blundered through the undergrowth. It was not only human enemies that the town walls kept out.

To the Briton still living in his mud and timber hut, Silchester with its 25-foot town wall, monumental gateway, and great public buildings, must have been an imposing sight, convincing him of the power and invincibility of Rome; but in fact town life on the Roman pattern and scale was barely kept up in Silchester, for the great buildings were expensive to build and maintain, and the native population was not so enthusiastic about

At the Butcher's.
(Photo: Mansell Collection)

the Roman way of life that it was willing to shoulder the financial burden involved. Most Britons in fact preferred to live in the country, and many of the richer people lived in great country houses, and only visited the towns when business made it essential. As a result, once the original enthusiasm for all things Roman had worn off, the towns gradually became more and more British; Silchester remained an important market town, and probably a considerable number of craftsmen still worked there but the citizens no longer had pride in their town. Whereas fine private houses still continued to be built, the great public buildings began to decay, and the roads were left rutted and unmended; only the public baths still continued to thrive. When the Western Roman Empire collapsed and barbarous Saxons occupied the surrounding countryside, town life in Silchester was slowly strangled, and today all that remains of the town is the wall. Corn now grows over the streets and house foundations of Roman Silchester.

A WALK ROUND THE TOWN

THE period of Silchester's greatest prosperity was the second century A.D. Let us take an imaginary walk through the streets of the town at this time, and try to gain some idea of the appearance and atmosphere of a typical Romano–British town.

It is market-day and the town is thronged with people who have brought in their cattle and pigs. Heavily-laden country wagons rumble through the crowds, their iron-shod wheels rutting the gravelled streets. A train of packhorses passes, each pony laden with barrels of oysters carried alive in splashing sea-water; they have travelled all the way from the Thames estuary. A slave carrying a heavy wine cask threatens to ram its iron rims into the faces of unwary passers-by.

These people that jostle together in the narrow streets and grind their hobnailed boots into sandalled feet are a motley crowd. Britain is a Roman province, but they talk and swear in their old Celtic tongue, and most wear the old British costume. One man with long hair and drooping moustaches strides by in a green cloak, scarlet tunic and yellow stockings; most dress in a far more humdrum fashion in rough undyed tunics. Nearly all wear heavy leather shoes or sandals studded with hobnails, and have baggy trousers cross-gartered with leather strips. Their faces are unshaven, and are burnt brown by the wind and the sun. Most of these country people have never had a bath in their lives, and they seem to belong to a different race to the sleek town magistrate who goes by in a litter carried by sturdy slaves. In truth, though, they are all Britons; it is not long since this magistrate's ancestors were fighting desperately against the Romans or leading head-hunting raids on their neighbours. Now, however, he considers himself a Roman, worships the Roman gods, baths every day, reads the Latin poets, and thinks it boorish to speak the old Celtic tongue. He wears the white cloak known as the toga. This garment is so cumbersome to wear, and so difficult to arrange with becoming grace, that in Rome itself the emperors have to pass laws to force the people to wear it even on ceremonial occasions. Here in Silchester, however, there is no necessity to pass laws, for the wearing of a toga in a British town marks a man out from the common herd.

The magistrate is indeed an important man, for he is one of only two senior magistrates who deal with all except very important civil and criminal cases (another two junior magistrates are responsible for the maintenance of the roads and public buildings), and when he retires at the end of his year's service he becomes a decurion, a member of the council which the Romans allow to control the affairs of the Atrebates. All the important tribes of Roman Britain have their own councils.

The magistrates try their cases in the town hall or BASILICA. This is a handsome building 232 feet long and 58 feet wide. It stands well over 40 feet high. Two rows of pillars divide this great hall into a NAVE and two aisles. The nave has semi-circular recesses at each end where the magistrates hold court, and has a higher roof than the AISLES; the wall opposite the entrance is pierced to allow admission to various offices and the chamber in which the town council meets.

The hypocaust system of heating houses.

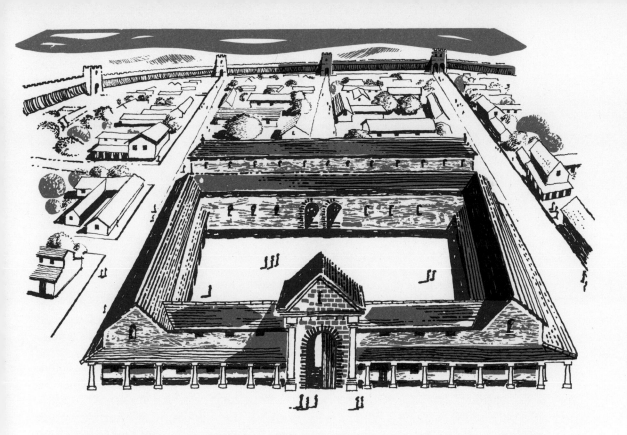

All the interior of the basilica glows with colour, for the thick, flint walls are covered with brightly painted plaster, and in places are lined with panels of expensive Italian marble. A mosaic of red and white tesserae (tiny cubes of stone or tile) covers the floor. The sunlight diffused by the thick, green-glass windows glistens on the bronze statue of the emperor, and picks out the painted statue of the tribe's patron goddess standing high above the gossiping, wrangling throng of people.

A small arched doorway leads from the basilica into the market-place or FORUM. This is a large gravelled square bounded on one side by the basilica, and on the other three sides by offices and shops with masonry counters and open fronts. Some of these shops sell fish and poultry, some meat, one does a roaring trade with its famous Colchester oysters. People jostle together in front of another which sells cheap, gaudy rings and brooches brilliant with red and blue enamels; it also sells crude statuettes of local gods and goddesses. Temporary stalls in the market-square sell fresh fruit and vegetables from the countryside, and one sells wreaths to worshippers celebrating the festival of one of the gods. The simple country-folk gape at the uncanny skill of jugglers and the daring of acrobats. Everywhere there is a hubbub of noise, as everyone haggles over prices and exchanges rumours and scandal. Above it all rises the quack-doctor's raucous voice advertising his very latest cure for all ills.

After the magistrate has finished his work he walks through the forum and goes out through the great gateway. We follow him, and after a short walk come to the public baths of Roman Silchester. The magistrate enters the dressing room where he strips off his dusty clothes. He passes quickly through the cold room (frigidarium) into the warm room (tepidarium) where he sits for a while chatting with a friend and begins to perspire. Before going into the next room, the hot room (caldarium), he puts on a pair of wooden-soled slippers, for the floor of the hot room is sometimes too hot for bare feet. In this room he sweats profusely and his slave, after rubbing him with olive oil, scrapes him down with a bronze instrument known as a strigil. This removes the oil and also all the dirt, dead skin and sweat. A quick splash in the hot bath, and he returns to the frigidarium, where he plunges into the cold bath and emerges glowing pink and feeling a much fitter and fresher man. He calls his slave, dresses, and goes to his home. There we will leave him.

In Rome itself one of the great baths covered over 30 acres (the whole of Silchester covered only 107 acres), and there rich and poor alike spent a great part of each day in the baths. In Rome, moreover, the baths were regarded not merely as a means of obtaining cleanliness but as social centres. The great baths of the Imperial capital were equipped not only with what we call Turkish baths, the normal type of Roman bath, but with swimming pools, running tracks, wrestling grounds and even libraries and museums. The townsfolk of Britain took whole-heartedly to this idea of combining cleanliness with recreation and every important town in Britain had its public baths; often they were amongst the most handsome buildings in the town. In Silchester itself the baths appear to have been among the first important buildings to have been built, and they were constantly used and freely altered during three hundred years of the Roman occupation. They did not have libraries and museums, but they did have a large courtyard which could be used by wrestlers, or by those playing a form of basketball or handball. In the dressing room, no doubt, men gambled and quarrelled over their dice games, played heads or tails with coins, or played chess or draughts with friends. Here, too, judging by the number of surgical instruments that have been found—scalpels, artery retractors and probes—the barber-surgeons of the town plied their trade. Seneca, the Roman writer and philosopher, says that the uproar was enough 'to make you hate your ears'; for the baths resounded with the smack and thud of the masseur's hand; the grunts and groans of those taking exercise; and the cries of the sausage-sellers or pastry-cooks. Piercing through everything else came the shrill call of the hair-plucker and the shrieks of his customers.

Both in Rome and Silchester the baths were heated by 'HYPOCAUST'—a Greek word meaning 'burning below'. Hot air from a furnace at the side of the building was allowed to penetrate into a space beneath a floor supported by short pillars. It then passed up the walls in vertical flue pipes. As a result both the floor and the wall radiated heat. It was a most effective form of heating, far more efficient than our open fires which send most of the heat straight up the chimney. When a few years ago experiments were made with a reconstructed hypocaust system it was found that a room temperature of 73° F. could be maintained after one and a half day's stoking, if the furnace was stoked twice a day. It is obvious that if the stoking was much heavier, the high temperatures necessary for the hot room of the bath-house could easily be attained.

TEMPLES AND GODS

WHILE the baths of the British cities looked after the bodies of the citizens, the numerous temples cared for their souls. In a few places in Britain these temples were of the normal classical type. At Colchester, for example, the Romans built a huge, rectangular, colonnaded temple, very similar to that of MARS the Avenger in Rome. (In this temple which was dedicated to Claudius, the Romans of Colchester made their last stand against

Boudicca's host.) But most British temples were similar to those built in Britain before the coming of the Romans. These had been made up of a squat timber tower surrounded by a verandah, both sometimes adorned with human heads, and a courtyard in which worshippers could congregate at time of festival. The Romano–Britons continued to build their temples in this form, simply replacing the timber by stone, and the heads by sculpture.

All the temples in Silchester were of this type. Two stood close together in a walled enclosure near the east gate. They were both square with a verandah around the tower-sanctuary, which was lighted by windows in the upper part of its walls. One temple had a floor of polished cement, the other, one of small red-tile tesserae. Probably both temples had domed ceilings covered by a pyramidal tiled roof; both had their flint walls plastered and painted a bright red.

Very little is known about the gods worshipped in these temples though in another temple south-east of the forum, a stone has been found bearing the word MARTI, and it has been suggested that the temple was dedicated to the Roman god Mars.

The Romans made no attempt to force the worship of gods like Mars on Britain, but to many Britons the success of the Roman army in Britain meant that the Roman gods were obviously superior to the native deities. When the Britons began to ape the Romans in manners and customs, well-to-do, ambitious young men probably thought it boorish to worship the old Celtic gods with barbarous names like Belatucadrus, Mapon, Toutates and Cocidius, some of whom were probably associated with human sacri-

Jupiter, a bronze statuette from Earith, Hunts.
(Photo: British Museum)

fice before the Romans came. (In Gaul the priests pleased Toutates by plunging a man's head in a cauldron of water until he suffocated.) In the towns and in the Roman camps and fortresses, Jupiter, Juno, Neptune, Vulcan, Mars, Mercury, Diana and other Roman gods were worshipped, and many more people worshipped the divine spirit of the emperor.

Probably, however, most of the poorer people in Britain (the great majority), especially in the countryside, remained faithful to the old gods. Often, when the nature and functions of a Roman and Celtic deity were thought to be the same, their names were linked together; Mars, the Roman war-god, in particular, was often associated with Celtic gods. This sometimes happened even when the functions of the deities differed, and then the hold of the native god on his worshippers was frequently so strong, that the Roman god merely lent his name and lost his original nature; Mars of all gods, for instance, became in some places a god of healing, in others a god of the wild. Frequently the British gods retained their original name and nature, and, what is more, often won over the

A temple.

Roman conqueror, for the Roman soldier always took care to keep on good terms with the gods of the country he was garrisoning. In the Balkans he worshipped a creature with the strange name of Zbelzardas, in Syria Dolichenus, and in Britain a varied assortment of mountain, river, and woodland deities. We find, for example, a junior Roman officer paying vows to COCIDIUS, the 'red one', probably a British war-god; he was also worshipped by men of all three legions. Near the Roman Wall-fort at CARRAWBURGH the water-nymph, COVENTINA, was worshipped, and a temple built over her sacred well; into this well the soldiers threw offerings of money and trinkets. At Bath, veterans, their gout-ridden and rheumatic limbs relieved by the hot springs, rendered thanks to Sulis, the presiding goddess. Anocitus and Maponus also had their devotees.

Throughout the Empire it was believed that the way to success lay through the proper honouring of gods like these. If a worshipper, using the right words, carefully and precisely performed the right sacrifices, and was scrupulous in fulfilling his vows, he expected that the gods would grant him his desire—a long life, riches, good harvest or the death of an enemy. It was a straight bargain between the god and himself, and the character of the worshipper—whether bad, cruel or good—made no difference to what was almost a commercial arrangement. Nor was it expected that emotion or fervour should vulgarize what was usually an austere and dignified ceremony.

As long as the Empire remained buoyant, and a reasonable number of requests were granted, faith in the old gods remained, but as the Empire slowly disintegrated, and the prospects of earthly success became much slighter, man began to turn to religions which compensated for the miseries of life on earth by the promise of a life in paradise after death. The two greatest of these religions, Mithraism and Christianity, will be described in another section.

24

HOUSES AND HOMES

THE temples and public buildings of Roman Silchester were well built with flint and concrete walls two to three feet thick; but not all buildings in the town were so solidly constructed. In the early days of Silchester many houses were made of timber with the chinks filled with clay, and even later there were not many houses with flint walls right up to the eaves. Throughout the history of the town most houses probably had a dwarf wall about two feet high, and above this a timber framework with a filling of wattle and daub (clay mixed with chopped straw, daubed on wicker hurdles). Many of these houses must have borne some resemblance to medieval half-timbered buildings.

Near the forum where land was precious, the shops and workshops of Silchester, their open fronts yawning at the passers-by, met almost gable to gable along the narrow streets, but normally the houses stood in ample grounds with orchards and gardens surrounding them. Some were actually farm-houses with barns, stables and byres into which the cattle from the town fields were perhaps driven at night.

The houses of the very rich inhabitants of Silchester—the great landowners—were well built and comfortable. They had wind-and-weather-proof flint walls two feet thick, plastered inside and out, and roofs covered with tiles to keep out the heaviest rain. Set in their large paddocks, many of these bungalow-type houses sprawled around garden-courts, gay at different times of the year with violets, foxgloves and dog-roses. Normally most of the windows overlooked these sheltered gardens, the houses often presenting a blind, unbroken wall to the noise and dirt of the street. A half-open verandah ran round the court, connecting the various rooms of the house. With the Roman green glass in their windows, and the hypocaust (see the section on the baths) heavily stoked, these houses must have been snug and pleasant to live in at any time of the year.

A Roman house.

Inside the houses were warm with colour. Painted plaster covered the walls, sometimes in a variety of colours which to us appear rather overwhelming. Often the upper part of a wall was divided into panels, which were filled with painted flowers, birds, animals or architectural scenes. (Archaeologists have found and pieced together a 12-foot length of painted plaster from St. Albans, which portrays in bright yellow, green and red, flowers, pheasants, and a leopard full-face.) The wall beneath these panels was often painted to resemble marble. Further colour was provided by mosaic floors made from tiny cubes of different coloured stones set in cement.

The rooms would be elegantly furnished with the couches on which Romans reclined at dinner parties, and with little three legged wine-tables. The legs of these tables, often carved into the shapes of fantastic creatures with claw-feet and tongues lolling out on their chests, were frequently made of slate-coloured Kimmeridge shale. Doubtless this furniture was kept well waxed and oiled by the household slaves.

In the bedrooms chests covered with mattresses served as beds, and held the best clothes of the family; other chests plated with bronze and iron, bolted into the concrete floor, and heavily padlocked, safeguarded its valuables. Besides these articles of furniture there would be folding stools with iron legs and leather seats, bookcases, cupboards, and perhaps a wicker armchair for the mistress of the house. Sometimes this furniture was inlaid with ivory or plated with bronze.

Normally rich Romans lavished much care and attention on their stomachs and the inadequacy of their kitchen equipment in Silchester is surprising. Only one oven was found when Silchester was excavated (of course there may have been more), and this was simply a large pot bedded in clay. Most of the cooking appears to have been done by burning charcoal under small gridirons which supported cooking-pots and pans. If this was the only method of cooking food, the people of Silchester must have done without baked meats, and have been content with fried or boiled food. Another surprising feature of these kitchens was their filthiness. Whereas the best rooms with the mosaics were usually kept clean, and were sometimes provided with drains to carry away water used to wash the floor, the gravel or earthen floors of the kitchens were often covered with several inches of debris—bones, broken pottery and decayed rushes.

Obviously Silchester's citizens, although they valued personal cleanliness, were not too worried about dirt and filth in their surroundings. This was typical of the Empire as a whole. Although Rome itself was provided with sewers so big that in places a wagon loaded with hay could be driven through them, most houses were not connected to the sewerage system; the city, which we think of as glistening with marble palaces and temples had many a dark, ill-smelling alley where people had to step warily around the open dung-pits. Most towns in Britain had no sewerage system at all. Silchester, in fact, was honey-combed with pits filled with refuse and waste which must have made the town an un-healthy place during hot summers. Moreover, Silchester, unlike some British towns, did not have a large AQUEDUCT to bring water to the town, and most of the town's water had to be raised from wells sunk through the gravel to underlying clay. There was, there-fore, never a plentiful supply of water to help to keep the town clean and healthy.

Diseases caused by the town's lack of effective sanitation must have affected all classes alike, but at least the rich, snug in their well-built houses, were protected against illnesses caused by the winter's damp and cold. We do not know much about the houses of the poor because all except very scanty traces of them have disappeared, but it is probable that they lived in huts with timber and clay walls and thatched roofs (probably leaky). Even those rather better off could not afford the expensive luxury of window glass, and they either had to sit and shiver while the winter wind whistled around their ears, or close the shutters and peer into a darkness relieved only by the feeble flames of olive-oil lamps or slender, dribbling candles. Not that they were kept warm even then, for most houses in the town did not have a hypocaust or wall-fireplace; Silchester's citizens must have relied largely on portable braziers, which leaked invisible but poisonous fumes, and gave off little heat. The death-rate from pneumonia and diseases like tuberculosis must have been high.

Still, what we have been describing was common in Britain only 150 years ago, and the people of Roman Silchester probably lived far more comfortably than their ancestors, or people in Britain for hundreds of years afterwards. Indeed the citizens of this quiet, picturesque, little town had many advantages over the inhabitants of the huge crowded cities of today with their bustle and noise, lethal traffic and poisoned air.

A silver skillet.
(Photo: British Museum)

THE GAMES OF THE ARENA

ONE more building of Roman Silchester should be described since it, like the public baths, was a regular feature of towns throughout the Empire. This was the AMPHITHEATRE, a circular, open-air arena in which fights between wild beasts and gladiators could be staged. In Italy and France, where amphitheatres were built of stone, many of them still survive, and in fact in France they are still sometimes used for bull-fighting. Britain, however, was a far poorer part of the Empire, and her towns could not afford to construct such solid and impressive buildings, with the result that today little remains of most British amphitheatres but a ring-mound covered with green turf.

The amphitheatre at Silchester has not been excavated, but its shape can still be discerned just to the north-east of the town. Its banks, which still stand to a height of about 18 feet, encircled an oval arena about 150 feet by 120 feet. In its prime it was probably very much like the amphitheatre outside the legionary fortress at Caerleon. This amphitheatre, which has been excavated, was slightly bigger than the one at Silchester, and had wooden seating for about 6,000 spectators. The seats were supported by a sloping bank of earth strengthened inside and out by a solid stone wall. In addition there were special boxes for the privileged.

Those amphitheatres outside the fortresses were used not only for sports and exercises but also for training the legionaries. On special occasions the legionaries flocked into the amphitheatre to watch displays of horsemanship and drill by picked bodies of men. These crack soldiers wore, not their ordinary armour, but scarlet or purple tunics, and carried vividly painted shields on their arms. Their silvered parade helmets carried yellow plumes, which waved in the air as they engaged each other in mock combat with wooden or blunted spears.

Towns like Silchester, however, were garrisoned by third-rate auxiliaries, and their amphitheatres were probably used for roughly the same purposes as those in Italy and France. We can imagine the townspeople urging on their claw-scarred dogs against the blindfolded bear or tethered bull, or cheering their favourite boxer as he smashed home blows with his brutal iron gloves. Silchester was probably too poor to enjoy the mass slaughter of animals (5,000 were once killed in one day in Rome's Colosseum), but occasionally its citizens may have seen trained prisoners of war fighting in the arena with sword and shield or trident and net. In Rome itself the people preferred the sight of men slaughtering one another to any other form of entertainment, and the Colosseum regularly resounded with shouts of 'slay!' from 40,000 throats.

To a people so brutalized as the Romans, however, even the gladiatorial games sometimes palled, and the emperors, who always gave the people what they wanted, varied the entertainment by dropping criminals into cages of hungry tigers, or exposing enemies who had fought too bravely to the attacks of other savage beasts. (A North African mosaic shows in vivid and horrible detail a Libyan charioteer, tied to his chariot, being savaged by a ferocious leopard.) Of all the great cities of the Empire, only Athens, still preserving a little of her true greatness, remained uncontaminated by this beastliness.

There is no doubt that the age was a tough and brutal one, but it is hard to think of any other people at this time or before, who were so drained of pity that they regarded the sight of men dying in agony as nothing but a splendid form of entertainment, so hypocritical that their educated classes tried to justify their enjoyment by stating that the combats of the arena were indispensable, because they taught the populace courage and contempt for pain. So devoted was the population of the Roman Empire to its blood sports, that it was nearly a century after Christianity had become the strongest religion of the Empire before the games were finally abolished. When we talk about the dignity of the Roman Empire, and try to weigh up what were its contributions to civilization, we must always bear in mind its coarseness, and the brutality it showed not only to those outside its bounds but often to its own citizens. Greek civilization, from which that of Rome was born, was, despite its outbursts of spontaneous cruelty, a far finer and nobler creation.

Gladiators.

SOME OTHER TOWNS

SILCHESTER will serve fairly well as an example of a tribal capital, but it is well worth noting that many other tribal centres differed greatly in their size. Caister-by-Norwich (Venta Icenorum), capital of the Iceni, whose land had been ravaged after their revolt, always remained an insignificant little market town, and Caerwent (Venta Silurum) in South Wales never covered more than 45 acres (compared with Silchester's 107). At the other extreme Cirencester (Corinium) capital of the Dobunni, covered 240 acres and was the second largest town in Britain.

Other tribal centres more nearly approached the standards of the normal Roman provincial town, in that they went somewhat further than Silchester in trying to ensure the comfort, well-being and happiness of their citizens. As a result of precise engineering, for example, water was carried to Dorchester (Durnovaria) in Dorset by an AQUEDUCT nine miles in length, and distributed to all parts of the town. (Roman engineers apparently tried to provide Leicester (Ratae) with a similar kind of duct, but failed owing to faulty surveying.) The supply of water brought to Wroxeter (Viroconium) from the Bell Brook was so ample that some of it could be used for cleansing the street gutters and flushing private latrines. Canterbury (Durovernum) and St. Albans (Verulamium) provided their citizens with stone-built, open-air theatres. All that is known about the former is that it had an outer wall 12 feet thick and an inner one 7 feet thick, but that of Verulamium has been fully exposed by excavation. Here there was a stage, dressing rooms, and an earthen bank on which wooden seating was placed. The stage, which had a slit into which the curtain could be lowered, was small, and it is probable that the audience more often watched bull- and bear-baiting in the pit than theatrical performances on the stage. In Rome itself the only popular tragedy was one in which the brigand-hero was actually put to death with tortures at the end of the play.

Usually those towns which were built for legionary veterans—Colchester, Lincoln, Gloucester, York—were not only more Roman in their planning and in the style of their buildings, but were better provided with the works of the Roman engineer. Lincoln provides the best example. Here the spring known as Roaring Meg was dammed, and a pumping station constructed next to the pool behind the dam. A double-action force pump, probably worked by slaves, was installed, and the water pumped the $1\frac{3}{4}$ miles to the town through tile pipes set in concrete. Lincoln, which was a flourishing town, was also provided with a covered fountain. Whereas, too, Silchester and most of the tribal capitals do not appear to have had a general sewerage system, Lincoln was provided with an extensive system of main sewers complete with manholes and tributaries. All these facilities were exceptional in Britain, and indeed the smaller towns, whether they grew up around forts or posting stations, or whether they were tiny market-centres, were usually unplanned and, except for the fact that their shops and houses were sometimes stoutly built, were little influenced by the example set by the big tribal centres or by the Roman colonies.

One more town must be described because it was unique in Britain. Not only was London by far the largest city in Britain and one of the largest north of the Alps, but it apparently continued to grow throughout the Occupation, and it has been estimated that in the fourth century its population may have reached 60,000. Nine out of ten people in most of the British towns were British, but the streets of London swarmed with Gauls, Greeks,

Syrians and Jews. (One out of every eight inscriptions found in Roman London refers to Greeks.) Their presence reveals to us the secret of London's prosperity, for these peoples were the great traders of the day.

As a result of their activities, by the time of Boudicca's revolt (A.D. 60) there was already a large sprawl of wooden shops and shacks along the Thames waterfront. This settlement was destroyed by Boudicca, and its successor was reduced to ashes as the result of a great fire during the reign of the Emperor Hadrian (117–38). But London prospered in spite of these disasters, and in fact could hardly help doing so, for no other town in Britain was situated in such an advantageous position. The wide Thames estuary engulfed the trade of northern Europe and channelled it down to London, from which the wooden bridge across the Thames and six great roads dispersed it throughout the province. The Thames and London's own river, the Walbrook, must have swarmed with the high-pooped, ungainly Roman ships.

London differed, moreover, from the other British towns not only in the fact that she was much bigger and her population so mixed, but also in the type and density of her buildings. Many of the city's inhabitants, it is true, lived in wattle-and-daub huts with thatched roofs; many others lived in somewhat more substantial buildings that sprawled in the Silchester fashion; but along the stone-paved main roads near the great basilica and forum, red-brick buildings stretched almost without a break, their large, arched doorways inviting passers-by into London's shops, offices and banks. Land here must have been precious, and some of these buildings may have shot upwards like miniature sky-scrapers. If they did, London alone of the British towns resembled the great cities of Italy and other more civilized parts of the Empire, where buildings over four storeys in height were common.

The busy waterfront of London.

London with its huge basilica (perhaps over 350 feet long), its tall buildings and high battlemented wall, must easily have been the most imposing city in Britain. Colchester was the original capital of the province, but it is extremely probable that this honour was soon usurped by London. At any rate London was important enough to be protected by a strong fort when the city rose anew after its destruction by Boudicca. Moreover a wooden writing tablet stamped (in the English translation) 'Issued by the Procurators of the province of Britain', shows that London was the seat of the provincial treasury, for the Imperial Procurator was the head of the province's financial service. In the fourth century, when the city was probably at its most prosperous, the emperor recognized its importance by conferring upon it the title of Augusta.

     *   *   *   *   *

Today little remains of the once thriving cities of Roman Britain. In a few places lonely and weathered pieces of wall still stand forlornly upright in the middle of a pleasant cornfield or, grimed with soot, among the buildings of a modern industrial town, but although these give us some idea of the massive strength of Roman public buildings, it is still very difficult to imagine what these buildings looked like in their prime. We have mentioned, for example, that some of London's buildings may have been several storeys high, but the only evidence for this is the great thickness of the foundations, which seems to indicate that they were meant to support multi-storey buildings either of brick or of stone; but that is not proof, and for all we know the buildings might have had only one half-timbered storey, and borne no resemblance to the great 'skyscrapers' of Italian towns. Occasionally however, as at Bath, the remains of a building are substantial enough to give us some idea of its original appearance.

Bath, a little town of 22 acres, had grown up around the great public baths, which in this case consisted of three swimming pools fed by hot springs, as well as the normal hot-air baths. Enough remains of these baths to show that here, at any rate, in Britain the Romans employed the engineering skill which besprinkled the Empire with magnificent buildings and great public works. A concrete vault 35 feet in span was thrown across the lead-lined Great Bath and its weight supported by massive piers, which in turn were buttressed by arches which led the stresses to earth. It is an example, on a minor scale, of Roman architecture at its most imposing, and there can be little doubt that if a tiny (though rich) town like Bath was provided with buildings of such grandeur, a city like London with its great wealth must have had many of a similar kind.

Another important discovery at Bath points out one other feature we miss when we stare rather blankly at Roman foundation walls and try to imagine what stood above them—nearly all Roman public buildings were adorned with sculptures and statues either in stone or bronze. At Bath the steep gable of a temple to SUL-MINERVA was richly decorated with carved tritons and winged maidens, and from their midst a gorgon's head with intertwining snakes in its hair and beard scowled down at the bathers in the Great Bath. Contact with Rome often blighted the native art of the Britons, but this head with its penetrating eyes, furrowed brows, and sweeping moustaches, is triumphantly Celtic, and when compared with Roman and Greek gorgons makes them appear very tame. If sculpture of this sort could be commissioned for this very civilized and fashionable little town, it is hard to imagine the far more British tribal capitals without some work of a similar kind. As yet it has not been found, but that does not mean it did not exist, and perhaps one day we shall have to revise our opinion that most British sculpture was merely a second-rate imitation of Roman work. It is well worth remembering, too, that though much of the sculpture produced in a Roman style by British sculptors may have been poor in quality, some very good work was imported direct from Italy, and a town as prosperous as London would almost certainly have been adorned with sculpture of this sort.

The Roman baths at Bath.

A Roman scythe.

THE VILLAS AND THE COUNTRYSIDE

MUCH has been said about the towns of Roman Britain because they were unique—neither before the conquest, nor for hundreds of years after the collapse of Roman power, was there anything like them in Britain. Their importance, however, is easily exaggerated; most of them, even the tribal capitals, were by our standards little more than large villages, mere specks on a largely savage and untamed landscape. In the north and west of Britain even small towns were very few, and here the countryside was largely untouched by man; swamp and forest covered large areas. Even in the south and east much of the country remained in this condition throughout the period of the Roman occupation. The road between London and Silchester was 45 miles long, but it had only one stopping place and anyone using the road crossed marshes and barren heaths, and travelled for miles through dank oak-forest thick with thorns and clutching brambles.

However not all the countryside was so wild. Large areas of forest had already been cleared for cultivation, for in Roman times, as in the time of our great-great-grandfathers, most people earned their living by working the soil. In the north these people lived in scattered and isolated villages, which remained practically untouched by the coming of the Romans. Here the cool, wet climate prevented the ripening of grain, and throughout the Roman period the farmers depended for their wealth on great herds of cattle. In the south and east agriculture was well under way by A.D. 43, and the Romans took over a going concern. Again there were few important changes. The Belgae from their lonely farmsteads had begun to clear some of the forest, and had ploughed some of the heavier soils, but on the whole the Britons had cultivated light or loamy soils, avoiding the heavy clays which were always difficult to plough. The Romano–Britons continued to live in isolated farm-houses, and largely farmed the same type of land.

Many of the British farmers profited little from the Roman occupation. Plagued by tax-collectors who sometimes took half of their crop, their young men conscripted into the army or forced to work on the roads, they had little reason to be grateful to Rome. In fact all that many poorer farmers could show as evidence of their new status as Romans was a nice red pot on a shelf, or some crudely painted plaster on the wall of their wattle-and-daub hut.

The great landowners fared differently. During the early years of the Occupation they continued to live in their rather squalid huts, but as the effects of the peace made themselves felt, many, encouraged by the Roman authorities, began to rebuild their old farm-houses or build entirely new ones in a rather more sumptuous fashion. Often, as at Lockleys near Welwyn, a rectangular house divided into rooms connected by a corridor, replaced the old circular hut. By the end of the second century many of these rectangular farm-houses had been enlarged by the addition of a corridor and wings to form what archaeologists and historians call the 'winged corridor' house. Tiles now replaced thatch, and the wattle-and-daub walls were covered with painted plaster. A concrete floor made the house clean underfoot—the pigs and chickens were pushed out of doors. In the yard outside stood well-constructed barns and byres. A large, solidly-built and comfortable farm-house of this type is known as a VILLA.

Villas of the 'winged corridor' type as well as many other varieties, were widespread throughout the south and east of Britain. Often they clustered around towns in which cattle, pigs, wheat and wool could be sold, and from which the landowners could obtain the few luxuries—wines, fine pottery, glassware, jewellery—to which they had become accustomed. Not that life was by any means luxurious in the villas for at least the first two centuries of Roman rule, for most villa owners went without the benefit of hypocausts and when the winter wind whistled under the tiles they rubbed their hands and shivered around charcoal braziers. There were few MOSAIC pavements. Not until the fourth century did growing prosperity lead to the erection of buildings that can be considered almost as comfortable and as imposing as one of our great country houses.

Until quite recently villas were often 'dug like potatoes', merely for their mosaic pavements or other interesting finds, with the result that we know very little about them. But, by putting together the knowledge we have gained from various sites, it is possible to obtain a fairly good picture of one of these houses.

The great villa stands snug in a Cotswold valley, clumps of trees protecting it from the westerly winds. Once it was a villa of the 'winged corridor' type, but a recent owner has extended the wings, and the long, low building now stretches round three sides of a courtyard laid out pleasantly with shrubs and flowers as a formal garden. A small statue of a dancing nymph forms a centre-piece. The fifty or so rooms of the house are connected by a corridor, and are lit by small windows high in their walls. There are separate rooms for summer and winter use, and the latter are now heated by hypocausts. In the centre of the largest summer room is a shallow water tank which helps to cool the air during hot summer days. Another much smaller room serves as a chapel, and contains an altar in front of which the family worships the household gods. Marble busts of the owner's ancestors stand frowning down from a platform. Several of the rooms are floored with mosaic pavements, a particularly fine one in the dining-room (triclinium) having been laid down by the Cirencester branch of a Greek firm with its main offices in London.

The house is eight or nine miles from the nearest town and so, unlike the houses of Silchester, it is equipped with its own baths. These are, of course, much smaller than the public baths of the towns, but they are laid out in much the same way with a dressing room and cold, warm, and hot rooms. Like the baths of the towns, too, they are hot-air baths with the heat provided by hypocausts. Unlike the rest of the building, which is half-timbered, they are built solidly of concrete, and are vaulted with a light stone called tufa, for the fierce heat of the furnaces would dry out woodwork and cause a fire. Just the same, as a double precaution, the baths are placed at the end of one wing, so that if any fire does break out it can easily be prevented from spreading to the rest of the building. At the end of the other wing of the villa there are the store-rooms and kitchens and, cut off by a wall across the corridor, the living quarters of the slaves. There are no hypocausts here and the floors are of earth or gravel. The kitchen is as dirty as those in Silchester, and has a large pit in one corner into which the garbage is thrown. Slops are emptied into a large earthenware jar.

Slaves work in the kitchen, clean and polish throughout the house, and also do much of the hard work on the villa lands. They sometimes work under the lash and their lives are short, but slaves are fairly plentiful, and if one dies he can easily be replaced. The slaves are usually bought full-grown, for if bought young they have to be fed

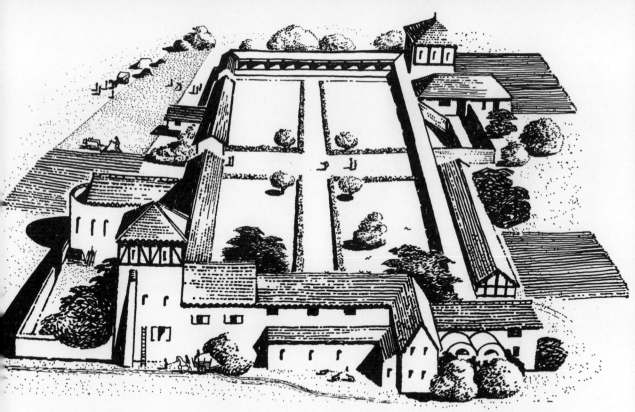

A large villa.

and clothed for many years before they become really useful. For this reason slaves are seldom allowed to rear their own children—in the outer courtyard of the villa are several small pits into which the bodies of babies have been thrust and lightly covered with soil.

The villa, although large and luxurious, is a working farm-house, and ranged round the same outer courtyard are its barns, byres and smithies. The largest barn is a thatched structure, with heavy buttresses propping its mellow, stone walls. Its wooden floor is supported by squat pillars, and is thus kept well away from contact with the damp earth. This is very important, for on the floor is stacked the wheat cut by the sickle, and any dampness could taint the crop with mildew. As an additional precaution (the climate is a wet one) the wheat is often dried over a crude form of hypocaust before it is stored in the barn. Wheat dried in this way is much more easily ground into fine flour between the massive, lava millstones.

A little corn is grown on the lands attached to the villa, but most of the wheat in the barn has been brought in by tenants as a part of their rent. Wheat yields are poor, and as little profit can be made from arable farming, much of the villa's land has been turned over to pasture. Cattle graze on the long, lush grass of the valley beside a stream. They are small animals and carry little meat, but their hides are in great demand, for the Roman army needs large quantities of leather for its 'BUTTERFLY' TENTS, and the jerkins, breeches and boots of the ordinary soldiers.

The short grass on the higher slopes of the hills is cropped by horned sheep. These are also small, and their meat is so tough that it is seldom eaten, but they produce fine

A Roman reaper.
The corn was pushed between the fixed blades.

fleeces, and British plaid blankets and waterproof woollen cloaks are famous throughout the Empire. Much of the villa's wool is woven into cloth and FULLED on the premises, but some has to be sent to the state weaving-mill at Winchester as part of the villa's taxes.

Despite taxation, however, enough profit was made from wool for British landowners to be able to erect large villas like the one just described. (Chedworth in Gloucestershire, North Leigh in Oxfordshire and Bignor in Sussex are good examples of these great fourth century villas.) Some of the tenant farmers with enough sheep may also have lived in small villas (there were some 550 of these compared with only 70 or so great villas), but most small farmers in Britain still lived in wattle-and-daub huts. These small farmers had to grow the food they needed, and therefore they could not afford to turn their arable lands into sheep pastures. They farmed small, squarish plots, the shapes of which can still be detected on the downlands of southern England.

Methods of farming were primitive. The Belgae had introduced a new plough with a large share and coulter (a long knife), which could turn a furrow and deal with heavy soils, and this was used throughout the Occupation. But at the same time, perhaps on the smaller, poorer farms, a plough was used which merely scratched the surface of the field, neither turning over nor burying the clod. This plough, therefore, could only be used on lighter, poorer soils. The Romans introduced scythes, but these were probably employed for mowing hay rather than corn, for they were very long and fragile. Most corn crops were cut with the sickle. Reaping machines, which tore off the ears and dropped them into a tray, may have been used on some large estates. Although there is no real evidence for them in Britain, they were used extensively on the great corn-lands just across the Channel, and it would be surprising if some great British landowners had not taken advantage of this invention. Fodder crops were not grown, and this meant that large numbers of cattle had to be slaughtered each autumn, because there would not be enough food to last them through the winter. Each year some of the land had to be left fallow in order that it might regain some fertility, for artificial fertilizers were of course unknown, and there was never enough manure for all the fields. Generally the Romans contributed little that was new to British farming—even corn-drying ovens and floors were in use long before the Roman conquest.

What did help farming in Britain was the peace that the Romans enforced, and their ability to organize great works of engineering. There was no longer the danger of raiding tribesmen driving off cattle and burning down buildings; now the great landowners could plan for the future, and build expensive barns and byres knowing that their children would reap the benefit of them. The roads that ran across Britain enabled the villas to send great quantities of corn and wool to the town markets and opened new areas of land to the British farmers. In the east of Britain Boudicca's defeated Iceni were set to work after A.D. 60 on a great scheme of dykes, canals and ditches to drain the water-logged Fens, and the Fens became, as they are today, the granary of Britain. The canals constructed served not only for drainage but for transport, and there is little doubt that

the people settled in these fens (which were probably state-owned) had the greater part of their corn
shipped away by the Roman authorities. A barge
could be loaded with corn at a wharf near Cambridge
and, using the Carr and Cnut Dykes and natural
waterways, could be pulled and pushed all the way
to the veterans' settlement at Lincoln. The Fosse
Dyke would then take the barge into the Trent, and
so into the Humber and up the Ouse to the headquarters of the Sixth Legion at York—a journey of
some 200 miles, and all by inland waterways. By
means of this great transport system the corn-lands
of the now fertile Fens were able to supply much
of the food required by the troops guarding the
northern frontier.

Grinding corn with a large quern.

SOME INDUSTRIES

TODAY when forests of factory chimneys cover large areas of Britain, and moths
have to turn grey to fit in with their scorched and blackened surroundings, it is hard
to realize that this is all the product of the last two hundred years. For the greater
part of man's history in Britain, industry was only of minor importance, and even during
the period of the Roman occupation by far the greater number of people were engaged in
agriculture.

But, during the time that Britain was a part of the Roman Empire, some industries at
least were organized on a large scale. The island had always been famous for its mineral
wealth—tin, lead and silver—and it was not long before these minerals were being
extracted from sites all over the country. Lead for example was mined in Flintshire,
Shropshire and Derbyshire. In the west of England the rich lead deposits of the Mendips
were seized upon as early as the reign of Claudius (A.D. 41–54), and the army was soon
organizing the export of ingots of this metal.

Lead was highly valued by the Romans because of the ease with which it could be beaten
out and shaped into pipes and vats, or the lining of baths. (The 80-foot long Great Bath
at Bath was lined with lead at 40 lb. per foot.) Mixed with the tin of Cornwall, moreover,
it formed pewter out of which mugs, tankards and dishes could be made. Above all it
contained silver, which could easily be extracted by smelting the lead over bone-ash
which absorbed the liquid lead, but left the silver on top in the form of tiny pellets. The
saturated bone-ash could then be re-smelted in a clay-lined hearth, and the molten lead
ladled out and cast into pigs marked 'from the Silverworks'. It was a wasteful process for
sometimes the slag contained up to 20–26 per cent. of lead.

Iron ore was mined and smelted in many areas of Britain, for great amounts of iron were
used by the army, and the growth in the number and size of farms led to a demand for
iron for scythes, sickles, axes, ploughshares and coulters. Many villas appear to have
smelted and even mined their own iron ore, but as vast quantities of wood were needed
to make the charcoal used in smelting, heavily-wooded regions like the Forest of Dean
(Gloucestershire) and the Weald of Sussex were the main centres of the industry. In fact

the production of the Weald field was so great that a large section of the Stane Street, which ran across the Weald on its way from London to Chichester, was paved with the cinders from nearby ironworks. Normally the iron produced was wrought iron, for it was difficult for the Romans with their crude bowl-furnaces to smelt the ore into a liquid, and they usually had to be content with a soggy mass which had to be hammered to remove the impurities. That is not to say that some of the iron eventually produced was not sometimes of fine quality; the cutting edge of a chisel recently recovered from the Walbrook was so hard that it could not be sharpened by a modern file. When well preserved, Roman tools could quite easily be put to use today, and often it is difficult to tell the difference between an axe, hammer or chisel made in the first century A.D., and one made in the twentieth century.

In at least one place in Britain the Romans mined gold. At Dolaucothy in the wilds of Carmarthenshire the veins of gold-bearing pyrites were followed by long, winding galleries. Some of these galleries were probably drained by water-wheels. These wheels kept the mine dry by scooping up water in boxes on their rims, and discharging it at a higher level into the sumps of other wheels, which in turn carried it to a still higher level. In the Roman copper mines at Rio Tinto in Spain there were eight pairs of these wheels arranged in a vertical sequence and together they raised the water nearly 100 feet. A similar system may well have been operated at Dolaucothy.

The galleries were cut through solid rock with the aid of sledge hammers and crow-bars. Occasionally, when a rock was particularly hard, fires were lit on its surface, and the red-hot rock suddenly cooled by dousing it with water. This had the effect of disintegrating the rock. Beams over ten feet long were sometimes used for propping the workings.

After the ore had been mined it was taken to the surface, crushed, and ground into a fine dust by rotary QUERNS. Water for washing the gold dust was brought to the mine by an aqueduct nine miles long.

Little is known about the people who worked at Dolaucothy. In many Roman mines the miners were slaves, who not only spent all their lives below ground but often died there.

38

Barges on a canal.

(In one of the Roman mines in DACIA archaeologists found the skeleton of a miner who had laid down to die on his rock-cut bench eighteen hundred years ago.) Probably some of the miners at Dolaucothy were slaves—those who turned the giant water-wheels almost certainly were—but the rest may have been free labourers, for at a short distance from the mines stood a fine bath-house, and it is unlikely that this was erected for the benefit of slaves.

The gold-mines of Dolaucothy are a good example of the Roman ability to scent out wealth in even remote regions, but it is doubtful whether the output of the mines was ever very great, and their contribution to the prosperity of Britain must have been small. What was more important to Britain was the far less exciting pottery industry.

During the early years of the Occupation most of the best pottery was imported from Gaul. This pottery, the fine, glossy-red ware usually known as SAMIAN, served as the best table-ware even in the households of the rich, and was so cherished by the poor that they carefully riveted together the pieces of any bowl or cup that had broken. Eventually, however, the flow of Samian ware began to diminish, especially after Gaul suffered severely from raids by German tribes in the third century, and its place was largely taken by pottery produced in Britain.

In the great kiln-yards at CASTOR on the Nene (near Peterborough) dark, lustrous pottery, especially drinking-cups, was produced in vast quantities, and transported to all parts of England. It was often decorated with scrolls of ivy leaves or, to suit the taste of the rich farmer, with hunting scenes of greyhounds chasing hares or deer. Sometimes the fights of the arena or chariot races were portrayed. This decoration was squeezed on to the pots in the form of semi-liquid clay, in much the same way as 'Merry Xmas' is written on a cake in icing sugar.

The pottery of Castor and other areas like the NEW FOREST, where wandering potters made a dark metallic-looking pottery with a white painted decoration, was fairly expensive table-ware; many other places produced much cheaper, coarse, heavy pottery—bowls, dishes, flagons and jars of various types—which served the everyday needs of most people in Britain.

Both types of pottery were fired in simple and rather crude baked-clay kilns. These were usually what archaeologists call up-draught kilns. This kind of kiln was made up of a domed oven set over a combustion chamber, which was connected by a short flue to the stoke-hole, the whole kiln being partly set in the earth. Fire-bars or a perforated floor supported the stacked pots.

When the fire was lit and pushed well into the flue, the heat and gases passed into the combustion chamber beneath the oven, and then into the oven and out through a hole in the dome. Firing having been completed the pots were removed by making a breach in the dome, which could easily be repaired with a plug of clay and straw.

The pottery industry was a flourishing one—after all, practically all vessels in everyday use had to be made of baked clay, for iron and bronze were expensive and beyond the pockets of many people. Moreover the towns and the army (over 50,000 strong) provided ready markets, which could easily be reached by means of the fine network of roads that covered the country. The Castor kiln-yards (where the owners or managers lived in sumptuous villas) even sent some of their beakers to the forts guarding the northern frontier.

On the whole, however, the advances made in the pottery industry and other industries during the years of the Occupation were surprisingly few—the only really big step forward being the introduction of the water-wheel, which could be used in flour-mills or saw-mills. Increased production was due more to the peace, and Roman ability to organize on a large scale, than to the introduction of new technical processes. Neither industry nor agriculture made the great step forward which would, for example, have enabled Britain to afford the expensive luxury of towns planned as centres of civilization.

Firing pottery.

HOW BRITONS BECAME ROMANS

OVER eighteen hundred years ago a Romano–Briton called Rufus took a wax covered tablet and with his iron STYLUS wrote (in the English translation).

> 'Rufus, son of Callisunus, Greetings to Epillicus and all his fellows. I believe you know I am very well. If you have made out the list please send. Look after everything carefully. See that you turn the slave girl into cash.'

On the outside of the tablet the address, London, is written.

The glimpse that this letter (lost in London's Walbrook) affords us of business life in Roman Britain is fascinating, but the style of the lettering in the original is even more interesting. The first sentence is reproduced on the opposite page.

This is Latin but the form of the lettering is different from any you will seen on monuments or in textbooks; for the letter is written in the ordinary flowing hand used by Romans to conduct their everyday affairs. Rufus, then, not only wrote Latin, but wrote it—not carefully and laboriously—but in the quick, practised hand of an expert.

But Rufus was a wealthy man and perhaps it is not surprising that he should write fluent Latin, for a knowledge of the language was essential to anyone in commerce or business. What is more surprising is that we find Latin written even by ordinary workmen. A tile-maker in London, angry with a fellow workman, scribbled, AUSTALIS DIBUS XIII VAGATUR SIB(I) COTIDIM (Austalis has been slipping off on his own every day for a fortnight). At Leicester another proudly wrote, PRIMUS FECIT X (Primus has made ten), and yet another at Silchester, obviously discontented scribbled, SATIS (enough!).

These graffiti, as the scribblings are called, are proof that even some workmen could read and write Latin. Some historians go even further, and claim that they prove that the same workmen spoke Latin as their normal tongue. This is, however, a completely different matter, for the workmen may have written in Latin simply because there was no British alphabet, and if they wrote at all they had to write in Latin. At home and chatting with their friends, however, the workmen may well have used the old British tongue.

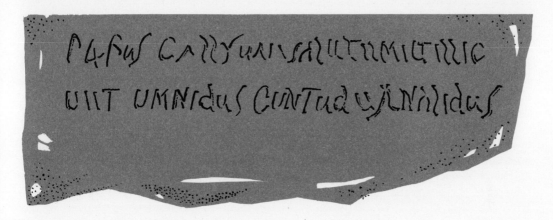

The Latin graffiti quoted all come from towns. Few inscriptions of any sort have been found in the countryside, and this may indicate that by far the greater part of the population there remained illiterate. Almost certainly most of the peasants seldom spoke Latin, for the Saxons picked up very few words of the language when they invaded the country in the fifth century.

However, the rich, both of the towns and the countryside, not only read and wrote Latin, but perhaps regarded it as their normal tongue. At any rate, as several mosaic pavements show, some wealthy Britons were by the fourth century deeply immersed in the Latin classics, and obviously expected their friends to have the same interests as themselves.

A mosaic at Lullingstone portrays the Greek hero BELLEROPHON and his winged horse, Pegasus, in the act of killing the CHIMAERA, which ineffectively vomits smoke and fire. In an adjacent room another mosaic has for its subject a scene from the story of Europa and Jupiter, chief of the gods.

Mighty JUPITER, so the story goes, fell in love with the beautiful EUROPA, daughter

A mosaic from St. Albans. A sea-god.

of a king of PHOENICIA, and wishing to take her away from her father, changed himself into a white bull and joined a herd which she and her maidens tended daily. Europa came down to the herd, which was grazing near the sea-shore, caressed the handsome, placid stranger, and seated herself idly on his back. The bull promptly rose, plunged into the sea, and swam to the island of Crete, where he changed into human shape and declared his love. Two of their children became kings and another a judge of the dead.

The mosaic depicts the bull on his way to Crete. He cleaves the water with powerful strokes, a rather smug Europa seated securely on his back. Above the picture runs a Latin couplet, a mild, educated little joke, which could only be understood by someone who had read the first book of Virgil's AENEID. Painted plaster and mosaics in other villas show that a knowledge of the works of Virgil was widespread.

The people who commissioned these paintings and mosaics lived in splendid villas, often built from the profits of their pastures. Their lives were leisurely and civilized, in many ways similar to those of the great landowners of Gaul and Italy. Their gods were the gods of Rome—sometimes with British characteristics—and when Christianity became the religion of the Empire Britain even managed to produce her own very spirited heretics. Even the dress of these fourth century Britons followed the fashions of the rest of the Empire. Eastern fashions were conquering Rome and they conquered Britain. On the wall of a Christian chapel at Lullingstone villa appear paintings of people clad in oriental-looking, beaded, and elaborately embroidered robes caught up by sashes; the dignified, austere, and very inconvenient toga has gone.

Life, even for these people, was short, but at least it was enjoyable. They hunted; took a gentlemanly interest in farming; delighted in intelligent conversation; occasionally visited the local town, squalid and dull by Roman standards, exciting in Britain; built well, and were proud of what they had built. To them Rome was, as the poet proclaimed, 'a Mother no Empress', and to them too the benefits of Rome rule were obvious: Britain had peace and her villas could sprawl unguarded throughout the land; great roads not only linked the cities but brought to the villas wine, glass-ware and fine pottery, and took away their wool, hides and wheat; industries flourished and brought wealth to many. These people were legally Roman; what is more they thought of themselves as Roman, and were often prepared to fight in order that Rome should be eternal.

Throughout the country, however, rich people were few, and a great gulf separated them from the mass of the population which often lived in a condition not very different from slavery. In the towns, perhaps, the craftsmen and shopkeepers were able to live fairly comfortable lives, but towns were few and small, and most Britons lived in the country-side where they could be easily bled by tax-collectors and vicious landlords. Justice was in the hands of the rich, and the poor were at their mercy. The poor peasant lived a life of drudgery now without even the occasional excitement of war. Men were probably far happier outside the bounds of the Empire.

As early as the second century there were risings of peasants in Gaul against the tyranny of their landlords, and in the third century the Roman army spent as much time fighting peasant rebels as German invaders. In the fourth century the Gallic peasants even caught and killed an emperor's brother-in-law. Intelligent people realized that the peasants had good cause for their discontent. When, in the fifth century, the German tide was sub-merging Gaul, a man called SALVIAN wrote:

> 'Are you surprised at not being able to defeat the Goth when even the Roman people of Gaul prefer to live with him than with you Romans? Are you surprised at seeing our towns captured and destroyed, when for a long time we have prepared for this disaster by the oppression of the ordinary people? When we reduced our fellow-citizens to slavery we prepared our own loss of liberty.'

He then goes on to say:

> 'What has in fact caused these peasant revolts? Is it not our wickedness, the criminality of our judges, their cruelty and corruption?'

What was true of Gaul was probably true of Britain, and when Britain likewise suffered invasion her landlords also found that they could not depend upon the support of the peasants. The Roman Empire meant nothing to the peasant, and he would do nothing to defend it.

YEARS OF DISASTER

THROUGHOUT most of the third century Britain, safe behind her Wall and protected by the sea, prospered. But all was not well in the rest of the Empire. In A.D. 256 the German tribes broke through the Rhine defences and plunged deep into Gaul, ravaging the country-side and burning the cities. At the same time other German tribes penetrated the line of the Danube and ranged through the Balkans; in the East the Persians defeated a Roman emperor and raided right across Asia Minor. The Empire seemed to be on the verge of collapse. In the end it was saved by a succession of vigorous and able emperors, who beat back the enemy on all fronts and recovered most of the lost territory; but the Empire had received a blow from which it never really recovered, and from then on Rome was always on the defensive.

Britain was too close to Gaul to go completely unscathed, and it was about this time that the Saxons from North Germany began to descend upon her coasts. These people rowed across the North Sea in their low, fast ships, and, coming in perhaps out of a fog, landed on a lonely shore, raided a villa or a small village, and embarked again before the Roman troops could catch them.

To hold back this menace from the sea the Romans had a strong fleet based on Boulogne in Gaul. It was largely made up of the long, slim triremes—galleys with three banks of oars—manned mainly by Gauls and Spaniards, but with some officers from further afield. (Saturninus, a captain of one of these galleys, came from a town near Carthage in North

Africa.) These triremes either ran down an enemy and smashed it with their ram, or they came alongside and captured it complete with its cargo of loot. The triremes were helped by large numbers of light, fast vessels (later often camouflaged to blend with the sea). Their job was to reconnoitre and report the presence of raiders to the main fleet. The fleet and the northern defences kept Britain free from all but small hit-and-run raids for the greater part of the third century.

In A.D. 286, however, the admiral of the Channel fleet revolted and proclaimed himself independent emperor of Britain. Civil war followed, and the northern garrison had to be withdrawn. For the first time in nearly a century the Picts swarmed south over the Wall; the fortresses of York and Chester were destroyed and savage bands of looters roamed freely throughout the countryside.

The revolt was eventually crushed by a general called CONSTANTIUS. He was a vigorous man, and soon followed up his success against the rebels by hunting down and destroying the invading tribesmen. Then the northern defences were rebuilt and York and Chester rose again, stately beside their rivers. Aware, too, that the Saxons were becoming as great a menace as the Picts, Constantius organized a system of coastal defences. The long stretch of coastline between the Wash and the Isle of Wight, the so-called Saxon Shore, was guarded by a series of massive forts; each protected an inlet or harbour from which vessels of the British fleet could sail to search the seas for the piratical row-boats of FRANKS and Saxons. Contingents of mailed cavalry based on the forts were to destroy any raiders who managed to elude the patrolling fleets.

There were probably ten of these great forts—Brancaster, Burgh Castle, Walton Castle, Bradwell, Reculver, Richborough, Dover, Lympne, Pevensey, Porchester. None of them bore any resemblance to the legionary forts and fortresses built during the earlier years of the Occupation. The early forts had been precise, rectangular structures defended merely by an earthen rampart with a stone skin. Little attempt had been made to plan their defences scientifically. The later Saxon Shore forts varied in shape—Pevensey was an irregular oval, Porchester square—and they were immensely strong. The walls of Porchester were still so strong when the Normans invaded Britain that they could serve as the outer defences of a castle; Richborough's walls of squared stones, flints and concrete still stand 25 feet high. In addition most of the forts were equipped with great semi-circular bastions on which heavy catapults could be mounted. These catapults were able to catch attackers in a cross-fire of deadly bolts, and could be swung to cover the whole length of the wall between the bastions.

In the west similar forts were built at Lancaster and Cardiff—the latter garrisoned by the Second Legion which had been moved from Caerleon. These forts guarded the north-west of Britain and southern Wales. Inland, new cavalry forts of the same type were built at Elslack (Yorkshire) and Piercebridge (Durham) to guard the Aire Gap and Teesdale.

At the same time many of the towns had their walls reinforced and equipped with the latest means of defence. The walls of Cirencester were strengthened by the addition of bastions, which blocked the flow of the stream that fed the wet ditch and created a stagnant marsh in front of the defences. Great Casterton, a little town on Ermine Street, had been protected by a stone rampart and a deep V-shaped ditch at the end of the second century; at the beginning of the fourth century the ditch was filled in and the wall reinforced with bastions, and at the same time a new flat ditch 60 feet wide was excavated out of the solid rock. Any enemy trying to rush these defences would come under a

The end of a Saxon raid.

The Saxon Shore fort at Porchester. The castle and church are medieval.

crippling fire, for every foot of the new ditch could be covered by the catapults mounted on the great bastions.

Britain at the beginning of the fourth century must have bristled with forts and fortified cities, and it is difficult for us to understand how any invader could make headway in a land so heavily defended. But forts and fortresses are only as strong as their garrisons, and are helpless without a strong field army in support. In the army there were some weaknesses.

In some ways the Roman army of the fourth century A.D. was more efficient than that of the first and second centuries. The use of artillery had been developed, and the catapult—which was used in open battle as well as siege warfare—was now far more powerful and effective. Moreover, one great weakness of the old Roman army had by this time almost been remedied. Although the legionary armies had been magnificent in battle they had always lacked the backing of a powerful cavalry, and as a result, now and again, they had suffered terrible defeats. The Roman government had in the end learnt its lesson, and by the fourth century strong cavalry contingents were in use as the striking arm of the army. Mailed from head to thigh and equipped with long spears, these horsemen charged knee to knee, and were almost irresistible in battle. Their dragon standards soon became feared by the enemies of Rome.

What then was wrong with the Roman army? One serious weakness was the fact that few men from Italy, and the more civilized parts of the Empire, now enlisted in the army, which was to an ever increasing extent made up of recruits from tribes beyond the frontiers. These tribesmen were superb natural fighters, but they would not endure the old type of discipline, and, as a result, they could not be so well trained as the old citizen armies. They refused to wear a heavy weight of body armour and preferred to wield the long,

46

slashing sword, the spatha, instead of the aggressive cut-and-thrust gladius. Often they enrolled under their tribal chieftains and fought with their traditional weapons—iron-clad ALANS with long, tempered swords, Franks with throwing-axes, and slant-eyed HUNS on shaggy ponies, with their fierce, bent-back bows.

It had always been the custom for Rome to recruit barbarians and civilize them by service in the army, but now so many of them were being enlisted that there was a grave danger that the armies would become completely barbarized, and out of sympathy with the provinces they were supposed to defend. Often invading Germans had to be fought by Germans loyal to the Empire, and there was always the chance that the latter might instead join in the plundering. If this happened there was no citizen-army that the Empire could fall back upon.

Perhaps it was treachery of this sort that led to the disasters of A.D. 367. Up to that year the defences of the province seem to have kept both the enemy from across the sea and from the north at bay; the villas flourished and Britain was prosperous. In A.D. 367, however, there was, as the Roman writers declared, a 'barbarian conspiracy'. Britain was attacked at the same time by all her old enemies. Picts swarmed over the Wall, and hundreds of these fierce little warriors in their curved skin boats slipped past the patrolling fleets, landed at night on a lonely beach, and joyfully looted villas and farms. Across the Irish Sea came the Scots, and from northern Germany and Holland savage Saxons and Franks. Britain's defences seem to have been swamped, and Picts were even able to roam at will in Kent. Villas and their crops went up in flames, and many slaves escaped to join the bands of looters. What was far worse both Nectaridus, who commanded the coastal garrisons, and Fullofaudes, the supreme commander, were killed and their forces routed.

Even with all their forces combined, there were probably never more than a few thousand barbarians in Britain, and it seems incredible that they should have been able to overrun the island so easily. They may of course have been helped. It is quite likely that some of the slaves and poorer peasants revolted, murdered their masters, and joined the invaders. It is known that some of the irregulars who guarded Hadrian's Wall conspired with the enemy in the hope of sharing the plunder, and something like this may well have happened in the south, where many of the garrisons were probably of German origin.

On the other hand the disaster may have been due simply to incompetence and in-efficiency on the part of the Roman high command—a fleet caught on the beach, cavalry

Roman cavalry of the fourth century A.D.

ambushed, forts taken by surprise. The field army only numbered some 2,500 cavalry and 3,000 infantry, and once this was destroyed there was no trained body of citizens to prevent the invaders roaming at will throughout the countryside. The fortified cities were safe, but the garrisons that manned their walls would be helpless to save the villas and farms that they saw blazing in the distance.

At length the Roman government awoke to the danger and sent Count THEODOSIUS, a very competent general, across the Channel with a large force. Theodosius had little difficulty in crushing the invaders, for they had split up into small bands that wandered around purposelessly, looting and burning everything in their path. The trained troops of Theodosius hunted them down and destroyed them as if they were so many wild beasts. What is more, to remind the offending tribesmen of the power and long arm of Rome, avenging fleets scoured the seas and ravaged tribal land as far north as the Orkneys.

Once law and order had been restored care was taken to prevent any recurrence of the disaster. Along the north-east and east coasts, and at some points in Devon, great fortified towers were constructed from which signals could be passed to the patrolling fleets. The northern frontier was guarded by tribes now brought into alliance with Rome.

Britain appeared stronger than ever before, but in reality she had been seriously weakened. Many villas survived the disasters of A.D. 367, and some were even built after this date, but many others had gone up in flames and others, deserted by their owners, stood desolate, their animals driven off and their crops destroyed, their walls slowly crumbling and silt drifting across the mosaic floors. Even when a villa survived the slaves had often fled and new slaves were by now expensive—the Romans were no longer conquering huge territories and selling their peoples into slavery. The villa owners were, as we saw, the part of the population most Roman in feeling and culture; now many of them were dead and many more impoverished. Moreover hundreds of peasants had either fled to the towns or had been killed, and the Roman government imported whole tribes of Germans to till the neglected land and protect the land they tilled. Britain after A.D. 367 was much less Roman, and from then on she began to slip at an ever increasing speed down the slope to barbarism. But this is going too far ahead and we must return now to the Britain of the early fourth century, safe and smugly prosperous behind her great fortifications.

The central medallion of the great dish from the Mildenhall treasure. It shows a sea-god. Roman silverware of the fourth century A.D.

THE SOLDIER'S GOD

THE centurion stepped out of the harsh light and dust of the street into the cool shade of the temple porch. Great double doors swung inwards, and he walked through a small, dark room and round a carved wooden screen, and descended several stone steps into the nave of the temple. The pungent smell of burning pine cones met his nostrils, and he could see the acrid smoke swirling up the narrow shafts of light to little windows set high in the gables. The lamp behind the sun-ray crown of a statue glowed dimly, throwing flickering shadows across the width of the nave and on to the benches on either side. On them he could make out the shapes of old familiar figures—the Raven, the Persian, the Soldier and several others. As the Raven showed him to his place on the bench, the centurion stared thoughtfully and with awe at the great marble altar-piece at the far end of the nave. On it had been carved the figure of a god, a magnificent young god, wearing a pointed cap and a flowing scarlet cloak. He half knelt, half sat on a great bull which struggled vainly to rise, as the god with one hand pulled back the animal's muzzle and with the other thrust a knife deep into its neck. The victor's face though stern was averted, as if he pitied the animal he was killing, but the marble torch-bearers on either side stood un-moved by the tragedy, one with his torch up, the other with his down. They represented life and death, and the god they accompanied was the great god MITHRAS.

Long ago, the centurion believed, Mithras had been created by the god of light, and after a miraculous birth to which had come wondering shepherds, he had slain a great bull from which had sprung all the useful living things of this world. Then, after protecting the world against the powers of darkness, Mithras, his disciples and his faithful ally, the Sun, had partaken of a last supper, and had been finally received into heaven.

Mithras was a noble god and Mithraism was very different from the state religion with its cold, formal bargaining between worshippers and gods who were indifferent to either wickedness or virtue; gods, moreover, who made no attempt to answer the question that had always troubled all men—what happened after death? People like the centurion knew the answer to that question, for had not Mithras shown by his own life that goodness prevailed, and to the just and upright came salvation and immortality?

A good soldier like the centurion was attracted by Mithras' demand that his worshippers should lead honourable and courageous lives; merchants and traders were attracted by the emphasis he laid on honesty and the sanctity of the plighted word, qualities on which their very livelihood depended. But even honourable and upright men could not feel ensured of immortality until they had passed various grades of initiation designed to provide proof of their steadfastness and valour.

In all there were seven steps in this ritual, each marked by a name: Raven, Bridegroom, Soldier, Lion, Persian, Courier of the Sun and Father—hence the costumed figures on the bench—and each grade was attained only after terrifying ordeals, during which the worshipper might be submitted to prolonged entombment, or led to think he was going to be burnt alive or drowned. At one stage, too, Mithraism seems to have taken over practices followed originally by worshippers of Cybele, the Syrian nature goddess. The worshipper knelt in a shallow pit partially covered with planks. A bull was led on to the planks and killed, and its blood flowed down over the worshipper and cleansed him of all sins, thus ensuring him a second birth.

Wherever the Roman army went Mithraism followed. Mithraic temples were thick along the Rhine where the legions faced the German tribes, and they have also been found in North Africa, Egypt, Syria, Asia Minor and the Balkans. In Britain the garrison of Hadrian's Wall built at least three of these little temples, and near London's Walbrook wealthy merchants and legionaries worshipped together in the fine temple which was excavated recently. But among the ordinary population converts to Mithraism were probably few. For many the Mithraic ritual was far too complicated, and the demands made by Mithras far too great—they preferred to seek an easier road to heaven. There were, too, no fiery Mithraic missionaries to strive to bring the unconverted into the fold. Mithras was worshipped by tight, smug, little groups convinced that they alone were saved, and quite willing to let the rest of the world be damned. Moreover worshippers of Mithras had none of the fierce, intolerant zeal possessed by Christians, and were quite willing to acknowledge the existence of other gods. Indeed statues of many different gods often shared a temple with Mithras. In the London temple the excavators found a fine head of Serapis, the Egyptian god of the harvest; a marble statuette of Mercury; a head of Minerva, goddess of wisdom; and a marble group representing Dionysus, the wine god, and his followers.

Mithraism, then, was a very tolerant religion, with none of the crusading zeal necessary to establish it as the state religion. Yet, of all the pagan religions, Mithraism was hated most by the rapidly growing numbers of Christians. You will perhaps have already noticed in the story of Mithras' life that there were some similarities between Mithraism and Christianity; Mithras like Jesus had a miraculous birth to which came shepherds bearing gifts, and like Jesus he partook of a last supper before ascending into heaven. In addition, worshippers of Mithras above the grade of Lion celebrated a ritual meal of bread and wine, which was compared with the Eucharist by horrified Christians; called

Mithras kills the Bull.

Sunday the Day of the Lord; and kept December 25 as a holy day. Christians, as a result, regarded Mithraism as nothing but a devilish mockery of their own religion, and attacked it unrelentingly. When, in the fourth century, Christianity became the official religion of the Empire, the Mithraic temples were everywhere overthrown, and their sculptures whole-heartedly smashed. Christianity thus destroyed a hated rival.

THE TRIUMPH OF CHRISTIANITY

ELEVEN years after he had crushed the revolt in Britain, Constantius added the title of emperor to the many others acquired in the course of a distinguished career. He barely had time to enjoy his triumph, however, for in the following year (A.D. 306) he died at York. His son CONSTANTINE, who had accompanied him on campaigns against the Picts, promptly proclaimed himself ruler of the Empire's western provinces, and was supported by Constantius' troops.

(Photo: Ashmolean Museum)

The Emperor Constantine.

The title of emperor was not hereditary, and Constantine found himself involved in a civil war with other generals who thought they had a better claim to the Empire. He crossed the Channel and marched on Rome, bringing his main opponent to battle at the Milvian Bridge (A.D. 312) just outside the walls of the capital. It was then that he was ordered in a dream to mark the monogram of Christ (more about this later) on the shields of his soldiers. He did so and his army swept their opponents from the field; thousands were killed on the battlefield or drowned in the Tiber. Constantine promptly gave thanks to God, for his victory convinced him that the god of the Christians had intervened on his side. Although he was not baptized until shortly before his death (and was still quite capable of murdering his own wife and son), Christianity, for the first time in the history of the Empire, was not only tolerated but actively encouraged. The numbers of Christians and the power of the Church grew rapidly, and by the middle of the fourth century emperors were forbidding the celebration of pagan sacrifices and the worship of idols on pain of death.

Christianity had triumphed; but the Christians had obtained their reward only after many years of hardship and danger. If Mithraism had not been a religion for weaklings, no more so had been Christianity. During the two and a half centuries before Constantine there had been no need for Christians to prove their courage by undergoing ordeals, it had required courage enough simply to admit that one was a Christian. For, in the opinion of most Romans, Christians were not like ordinary, decent people: they kept themselves to themselves; they would not acknowledge the existence of other gods (the mobs yelled, atheist!); they even refused to sacrifice to the emperors, and were thus guilty of treason. During the early years of the Empire, then, Christians were unpopular, and suspected of all sorts of abominable practices. It was with general approval that they were harried by the emperors; Nero nailed them to crosses or burnt them alive, and every now and then succeeding emperors in moments of panic, or alarmed by their growing numbers, ordered fresh executions. It was during one of these persecutions (probably at the beginning of the fourth century) that St. Alban was beheaded on the hill where St. Albans Abbey now stands. His courage in refusing to give up his faith was paralleled by hundreds of nameless martyrs, and their steadfastness in the end won the admiration of pagans, and converted many to Christianity.

With the conversion of Constantine all persecution ceased, and Christianity spread rapidly throughout the eastern part of the Empire. In the western provinces, however, progress was much slower. The peasants of Gaul, for example, remained resolutely pagan until the end of the fourth century, and were only converted by the crusading zeal of ST. MARTIN, who (sometimes supported by soldiers) threw down pagan statues and temples and erected churches in their place. Britain was even more backward. Right at the end of the fourth century a fine temple to NODENS, a god of healing, was built on a hill-top on the northern side of the Severn estuary, and this flourished till well into the fifth century. A smaller temple was built at the same time within the ramparts of the now deserted Maiden Castle. Perhaps even at this date Christianity was still largely confined to the miserably poor of the towns. It is true that Britain sent three bishops to a meeting of clergy at Ariminum in northern Italy (A.D. 360) but their congregations were so small and impoverished that they could not afford to pay their bishops' travelling expenses, and these bishops, alone of the four hundred delegates present, had to be helped by a grant from the imperial treasury.

Just how many Christians there were in Britain at this time we shall never know, but there was at least a sprinkling of them all over the country, for numbers of articles have been found inscribed with Christian signs. Sometimes a bowl, dish or cup has scratched upon it the fish, the Greek word for which was taken to mean, Jesus Christ Son of God, more often it is the Chi-Rho monogram ℞ , formed from the first two letters of the Greek word for Christ. It has been claimed, too, that small buildings at Caerwent and Silchester were Christian chapels, but there is not much reliable evidence to support this assertion, and until quite recently no definite place of

An early Christian church: in front a standard showing the Chi-Rho.

Christian worship dating to Roman times had been discovered. Then, about ten years ago, excavations at Lullingstone villa in Kent, recovered wall plaster on which had been painted the richly dressed figures described previously. These figures had their arms outstretched in an attitude which suggested the early Christian at prayer. A year later patient work on some of the other plaster revealed a large wreath (three feet in diameter) enclosing a bright red Chi-Rho. Wall paintings of this type make it highly probable that at least a part of the villa was used as a Christian chapel. If it was, it is the earliest place of Christian worship that has yet been found in Britain.

Here at Lullingstone, then, was one landowner who was so fervent a Christian (as early as A.D. 350) that he was prepared to adapt a part of his villa for use in Christian worship. As time went on, and Christianity became increasingly respectable, more and more of the landowners became Christians. Many found that the Christian Church offered an attractive career to men of ability, and the ranks of the upper clergy soon became filled with the younger sons of the great landowners. As Britain slipped slowly into barbarism, moreover, Christianity began to win over the peasant masses, who must have found in the prospect of immortality some consolation for the misery of their life on earth. Christianity made headway, too, among people beyond the bounds of the Roman province. ST. NINIAN and ST. PATRICK took the word of God to Scotland and Ireland, and there it survived and flourished, even when the pagan Saxons had swarmed across lowland Britain, and broken the island's last link with Rome.

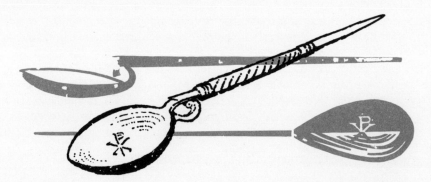

Roman spoons showing the Chi-Rho.

THE END OF ROMAN BRITAIN

ROMAN historians tell us very little about the last years of Roman rule in Britain, and for our knowledge of this period we have to rely largely upon Saxon records, which are very patchy and often inaccurate. Even archaeology cannot tell us much, for much of the late Roman material was not buried, and was often re-used by later peoples, whilst the timber houses of the early Saxon villages have long since decayed and are difficult to trace. As a result we have to build up our picture of this period by fitting together the tiny pieces of evidence obtained from inaccurate records and the contents of Roman and Saxon graves. It is like trying to make out the picture on a jig-saw, when nine-tenths of the pieces are missing and the others do not fully interlock.

It is not surprising that archaeologists and historians join up the pieces in different ways to form different pictures, and in fact while some are disagreeing about the dates

The Barbarian Invasions

of important events in this period, others are just as vigorously denying that those events took place at all. What we have to say in the last part of this book, then, is based on insufficient evidence, and may quite possibly be inaccurate or even completely wrong. All that can be said for it is that it represents the opinions of some modern archaeologists and historians.

The Picts and Scots were quiet for a while after Theodosius had harried them in A.D. 368, but soon they were on the move again, probing the Roman defences, slipping past the forts on a dark night, burning and looting defenceless farms and villages. In A.D. 383 they overran and destroyed Hadrian's Wall and this time it was not restored. According to archaeologists the Yorkshire signal stations suffered the same fate in the nineties. At Huntcliff in the north, bones of men and women were thrown into a well; at Goldsborough a short, thick-set man fell face-downwards across an open hearth, stabbed in the back. Near his feet lay the skeleton of a tall man with the skeleton of a large dog, its head against his throat. Perhaps Picts or Saxons came in under cover of a sea-fog, rushed the gates, and massacred an unprepared garrison; perhaps the death of one Briton was avenged by a large dog.

Rome could do little to help Britain. In A.D. 378 the Imperial Army had suffered one of the worst defeats in its history, when at Adrianople the Roman infantry, pressing forward to victory, was caught in the flank and butchered by the Gothic cavalry. From then on Rome herself was always struggling, and found it difficult enough to defend the richer parts of her empire, without bothering about a backward, isolated province like Britain. The position was made even worse when in A.D. 406 hordes of Germans crossed the frozen Rhine, overwhelmed the frontier defences, and plunged deep into Gaul. At the same time other German tribes plundered the Balkans and entered Italy, sacking Rome itself in A.D. 410. Troops had to be withdrawn from Britain, and the British cities were told that they would have to arrange for their own defence. No doubt both the Romans and the Britons thought this a purely temporary measure, only in force until there were sufficient troops available to re-occupy the province. But there never were enough troops available, and from A.D. 410 onwards Britain had to fend for herself. (Some historians think that the Romans re-united the province with the Empire for a few years in the second decade of the century.)

On the whole Britain seems to have looked after herself fairly well. It is true the Picts still remained a menace, but the Saxons do not seem to have caused so much trouble, and the Scots appear to have stopped raiding about this time, perhaps because they had been converted to Christianity by St. Patrick. As a result Britain was reasonably prosperous. She was no longer a part of the Empire and few of her people were Roman in thought or feeling; her roads were rutted and pot-holed; her centres of industry were destroyed; but nothing could harm the rich soil of her lowlands, and as long as men were allowed to grow and reap their crops (now untaxed by a central government) Britain could not help enjoying a crude plenty.

But there is no happy ending to the story of Roman Britain. In A.D. 441 there occurred a raid by Picts and Saxons, which caused widespread damage throughout the country. The local leaders (who were probably the city magistrates) were helpless, and in despair appealed to AETIUS the Roman commander in Gaul for help. 'The barbarians,' they complained, 'drive us back to the sea, the sea drives us back on the barbarians. We can only choose between two kinds of death, to be slaughtered or to be drowned.' But Aetius' troops were trying to throw back an invasion of Huns, and he was unable to send an army to Britain. In the end, desperate, the Britons called in the help of a local king in Wales, a man called Vortigern.

The Anglo-Saxon historian, BEDE, tells us that VORTIGERN tried to play off one set of invaders against the other; Saxons from north Germany were invited to Britain and given land in Kent on condition that they protected Britain against all her enemies. But these Saxons were a barbarous people and had no intention of keeping their part of the agreement. Suddenly they revolted and attacked their British allies, whilst at the same time their kinsfolk came swarming across the North Sea in their long row-boats. Then, according to Bede, followed a period of terror. The Saxons ranged throughout Britain without opposition: 'public and private buildings were razed; priests were slain at the altar; bishops and people alike, regardless of rank, were destroyed with fire and sword, and none remained to bury those who had suffered a cruel death.' Survivors eked out a miserable existence amongst the hills, forests and swamps. All because Vortigern had foolishly invited treacherous Saxons to Britain.

But Vortigern is wrongly cast as a fool or villain. When he called in one tribe of barbarians to fight other barbarians, he was following a traditional Roman practice. Even before A.D. 367 the Saxon Shore forts were probably garrisoned by Germans, and after the devastation caused by the raids in that year, more were brought across to Britain to till and defend the deserted lands. About A.D. 400 too, groups of German spearmen were planted in positions suitable for defence—at important road junctions and outside the gates of important towns like Colchester, York, Lincoln and Corbridge. As a result, some historians think, the greater part of the population in eastern Britain was already speaking German by the time Vortigern brought across his Saxon mercenaries. Vortigern, then, was was not so much criminally foolish as unlucky, in that the barbarians he brought across were more treacherous than most.

Nor were the results of Vortigern's invitation quite so terrible as Bede makes them out to be. It is true that it led to the Saxon conquest but that took hundreds of years and would have come anyhow; and as for the widespread damage that Bede describes—

all that can be said is that archaeology shows little evidence of it. A few places were plundered. At Caistor-by-Norwich excavation revealed thirty-two skeletons in a burned down house, and this town was probably sacked (perhaps by the very spearmen who were supposed to protect it). We know too from the Saxon histories, that when AELLE and his Saxons captured the Saxon Shore fort of Pevensey, they 'slew all who dwelt in it, nor was there one Briton left'. But the larger cities were impregnable and could not have been taken at this time.

What then did happen to the Roman towns? In the first place there was probably little that was Roman about them after the middle of the fifth century. Most of the public buildings—town hall, temples, baths—had fallen into ruin, streets were rutted and the walls crumbling. A few craftsmen remained, but most of the thatched huts were inhabited by people who struggled to earn their living by cultivating the lands outside the town walls. The Saxons, who were farmers, were not interested in the towns and simply ignored them, but they were interested in land; in their search for new farmlands they spread steadily westwards, not only cutting off all trade from the British towns and severing their last links with the Continent, but also depriving them of the lands needed to feed their people. Most towns, then, did not go up in flames, whilst barbarians with horned helmets chased screaming women and children through the streets, but slowly, miserably, faded away, until their last inhabitants deserted them, and their buildings simply fell to pieces.

By the end of the sixth century people of German stock had occupied most of low-land Britain. The ghost towns of Roman Britain stood forlorn, buildings crumbling, roofs fallen in, roads half blocked by the ruins of houses. The Saxon minstrel wandering among the ruins of Bath marvelled at the 'wallstone broken by fate', and later, by the great fire of his lord's hall, told his audience how the work of giants was decaying—towers were ruined, gates rotted, cement and stone were crumbling. In the countryside the great villas (ignored by the new owners of the land) stood unoccupied, the wind blowing through their doorless rooms, weeds pushing up their mosaic floors.

Nor did the Saxons retain many other features of the great Roman civilization. Wild and fiercely independent, living in primitive and isolated villages, they could not be organized or controlled by any central government, and in fact when they were not fighting the Britons they were usually fighting one another. With no one to order (or wish) their repair, the rutted, pot-holed roads soon became overgrown with weeds and bushes; the rotten timbers of the bridges fell and blocked the streams. In the east the once fertile Fens became swamps, the homes of desperate Britons, who every now and then emerged to rob and kill the people who had stolen their land. Memories of Rome remained, but these were faint and confused, and in some places even these had disappeared. In the lowlands even Christianity wilted before Woden, Thor and Tiw, the Saxon gods, and although it survived in the unconquered west, the Britons made no attempt to convert their oppressors. Britain may have gained a new, vigorous stock of efficient farmers, but for many generations the island was cut off from what remained of Roman culture, and as a result the general level of her civilization fell well below that of Belgic Britain. Not until AUGUSTINE and his missionaries landed in Kent at the end of the sixth century, was Britain again brought into the main-stream of European civilization.

Picts swarm ashore.

GLOSSARY AND INDEX

A list of words which are to be found in the book together with their meaning.

CARLISLE

HADRIAN'S WALL

CORBRIDGE

YORK

ROMAN BRITAIN

THE MAP SHOWS A NUMBER OF IMPORTANT
PLACES MENTIONED IN THE TEXT